Wisdom
of
Sri Sri Ravi Shankar

Wisdom of Sri Sri Ravi Shankar

Ed. Karishma Bajaj

Ocean Books Pvt. Ltd.

ISO 9001:2008 Publishers

Published by
Ocean Books (P) Ltd.
4/19 Asaf Ali Road,
New Delhi-110 002 (INDIA)
e-mail: info@oceanbooks.in

ISBN 978-81-8430-243-1
Wisdom of Sri Sri Ravi Shankar
Ed. Karishma Bajaj

Edition
First, 2013

Price
Rs. 300.00 (Rs. Three Hundred only)

Printed at
Bhanu Printers, Delhi

Contents

Dedication

A Guru is the One who dispels darkness from your life and leads you to the light of your very being.
A Guru is the Enlightened One who leads you to your Self.
A Guru is the One who is your very path to reach your destination.
A Guru is the One who leads you to Unconditional Love, which is the core of your being.
A Guru is the One who peels away the layers and the layers that covers your spirit.
A Guru is the One who wipes away all the deeply ingrained impressions that blur your divine vision.
A Guru is the One who collects all your garbage, carries your burdens and wipes your tears in return for your happiness.
A Guru is the One who awakens the child within you bringing you back to your own nature.
A Guru is the One who gives you everything for nothing in return.
A Guru is the One who gives you knowledge, creates experience and opens the doors of wisdom.
A Guru is the One who carries you across the sea of karma to the shores of God-Realisation.
A Guru is the One and the only One who awakens the Guru within You...

This is my Guru

Acknowledgments

I thank Guruji, for you have dispelled my darkness and led me to the Light within me – My Self – Divinity.

I thank God – the Universe, for sustaining my life, while I am on my journey here.

I thank my Angels, for being with me, every moment of my life.

I thank my father, for you have been instrumental in leading me onto the path of spirituality, guiding at every stage and helping me evolve.

I thank Girish, for you have taught love, patience and trust by simply being you. You have brought out the best in me and continue to do so.

I thank Mr. Piyush Kalam, for you have given me the opportunity to compile this book.

Editor's Note

It was during the journey of compiling the *Wisdom of Sri Sri Ravi Shankar* by Sri Sri Ravi Shankar that I had the opportunity to rediscover my Guru. The *Wisdom of Sri Sri Ravi Shankar* compiled in this book have led me back to the journey of discovering my Self NOW!

As I re-visited the precious words spoken by Guruji, as lovingly address Him, I felt as though I was not accumulating knowledge, but letting go of all that I held onto. Some Notes I just kept re-reading till something dawned within me. I experienced the sparks of light within me that did not seem to exist till this book happens.

I actually came to understand what great Masters of the past and the present mean when they say that when wisdom dawns you gain nothing, but lose everything. You lose all those negative thoughts, emotions and feelings. You lose all those impressions that clouded your divine vision. You lose those layers and the layers that have piled up through years and years. You lose all that is 'mine' and gain all that is 'I'.

Yes, when a master like Guruji shares with us the Notes of Wisdom, He is actually giving us an opportunity to lose ourselves to find Myself. He leads us to Self-Realisation and God-Realisation. He makes you come into awareness about the true purpose of your life, effortlessly.

Each Note compiled in this book is a precious treasure, which makes the seeker's journey invaluable.

Compiling this book *Wisdom of Sri Sri Ravi Shankar*, has brought me to MySelf, and I wish every person who reads these Notes experiences the flow of Guru's Grace into his life.

Thank You Guruji for the most precious Note: "To that Divinity

within me, which is Me; to that Divinity I surrender." Your magical words have transformed me... May these words transform everyone. May these words help everyone find the divinity that exists within him/her. May these words help everyone find You in him/her and him/her in You...

The Secret of the *Wisdom of Sri Sri Ravi Shankar* is that they bring you into the NOW… It is only NOW that you live. And as you read each Note, you become aware of the importance of being NOW in the NOW… The past was your destiny, the future is an illusion till it happens. NOW is who and where you are. When you become aware of this secret… stress, fear, worries, anxieties, insecurities, anger, hatred, etc. drop away and become one with your Self… You are naturally happy, in love with love, compassionate, peaceful, blissful, content, etc.

The Guru's blessing of Surrender, Unconditional Love, Happiness, Prosperity, Happiness, Peace and Bliss will always be with you NOW!

Introduction

No matter how many words you use to describe Sri Sri Ravi Shankar, they are too less. Guruji, as He is lovingly known by His devotees across the world is considered to be a phenomenon, who has changed peoples' lives. He has come to serve the world and He does just that. He travels across places bringing smiles to thousands of people each day.

In all the years that I have been a part of the Art of Living Foundation, and having spent quality time with the Master, I have seen Him blessing people unconditionally. He has spent sleepless nights interacting with people, travelling, healing, blessing, guiding. The Art of Living Foundation, which He founded, has actually taught millions of people across the world the actual Art of Living.

There have been cases when people going through mental, emotional and physical ailments have been cured. There have been prisoners reformed. There have been youth brought onto the path of spirituality and career, children excelling. Guruji has touched millions of lives directly and indirectly.

Guruji has brought miracles to people through the gift of the Sudarshan Kriya – a breathing technique that has magically changed lives. This technique when practised regularly returns smiles and eliminates stress. Apart from this there are varied courses designed to heal people from all walks of lifes, across the varied age-groups.

Guruji conducts knowledge sessions every evening, no matter where He may be in the world. He has brought back age-old knowledge, simplified it and presented it to people, transforming their lives. He explains what may seem complex concepts in the simplest way possible. The Knowledge Notes given by Him to people have lit the light of wisdom in him/her. Many have realised the self through these precious

treasures of wisdom.

He has given discourses on important texts such as the *Bhagwad Gita*, the *Ashtavakra Gita*, the *Patanjali Yogasutras*, the *Narada Bhakti Sutras*, the *Shiv Sutras*, etc. He has spoken extensively on subjects such as devotion, surrender, peace, love, enlightenment, etc. His *Wisdom of Sri Sri Ravi Shankar* have led millions to befriend the Divinity within him/her and around him/her. They have met the Divinity that they have been searching for.

Through Satsang sessions Guruji has brought celebration into life. It is a part of spiritual progress and evolution. There are satsangs held in every part of the world – small groups gather weekly singing devotional songs and sharing Guruji's knowledge. According to Guruji celebration and smiles are the reason we are here... It is our basic nature to be joyful.

Guruji has led millions of people onto the path of Seva (Service). Seva towards humanity in order to spread peace, love and harmony, in order to break down the wall between borders. Devotees across the world have contributed towards making the Art of Living one of the largest Non-Government Organisations of the world. Hundreds of projects have been initiated under the wings of Guruji, which have been executed by devotees, thereby uplifting millions of life. Villages have been adopted, prisoners have been reformed, addicts have been rehabilitated, orphans have been adopted, trauma relief has been provided, areas rebuilt... so much continues to be done today by each devotee.

Sudarshan Kriya, Satsang, Seva have brought smiles to millions of people in over 150 countries. Guruji continues tirelessly and effortlessly to spread smiles. They achieve Self-realisation so that people may achieve their purposes of life and God-realization.

Guruji magically awakens Divinity in each Devotee, so simply...

An introduction to Guruji's *Wisdom of Sri Sri Ravi Shankar*, with a Note on God:

God is never an object of isolation but the very core of your being. The difference between Self and God is just like the wave and the ocean. Can there be a wave without the ocean?

Who are you? Do you know about yourself? Find out about

yourself first. If you think you are just the body that is not possible because the body has its limitations. If you think that you are the mind then is also not possible because the mind too has its limitations. It is just another layer of our existence. If you know that you are Silence or that you are Space, then it is possible God is also Space.

Just like your body is made up of proteins, amino acids and carbohydrates, your mind and soul are made up of love. You are made up of love. Everyone is full of love and love is God. So you are made up of God! Every little atom of your body is made up of love and that is what is God. Do not think that God is sitting somewhere in heaven. God is here and now!

God is not somebody with a big white beard, sitting in heaven. God is love. He is Space. When you are meditating, when you feel at peace, at home with everyone, you are in touch with the Divine force. Can you live without love? In the Upanishads, it is said *kham kham brahma* – the Space is God, in which everything is and into which everything dissolves.

What is not God? What is the definition of God, if at all there is one? You describe it as that which is everywhere; which is all-powerful, which is responsible for this creation, for its maintenance, and for its dissolution; which is Omnipresent, Omnipotent, and Omniscient. You say, "I want to see God." When you want to see God as something, as an object, then it is not everywhere. Then you are not God. This desire to see God as separate from you is also an illusion. God is not an object of senses, but the feeling of feelings, the presence of presence, the sound of silence, the light of life, the essence of the world and the taste of bliss.

Just as love is felt in the heart, so is God's presence felt. God is never an object of isolation. God is the sum totality. When you dissolve, God remains. When you are there, there is no God. Either you can be there, or God can be there, not both. So when you meditate, you become one with God. You are God. That is why it is said, 'Tat tvam asi', meaning, 'Thou art that.'

God is to be felt in the depth of your heart. God can neither be perceived through your senses nor through the mind. God is the seer

Himself. Who sees? That is God. Space is God. Space is everywhere, and everything is in Space. Nothing can touch Space. Nothing can destroy Space. And you cannot see Space as a separate object.

□

Wisdom of Sri Sri Ravi Shankar

Love is seeing God in those next to us,
Meditation is seeing God within us.

A wise person makes no effort to conceal a secret. But he does not make an effort to reveal a secret either. For example, you do not talk about menstruation, death, etc. to a five-year-old boy/girl, but as he/she grows older these things are not hidden from him/her any more. These concept become known as a matter of course.

An unenlightened one tries to protect a secret; and he also reveals the secret at the wrong time, to the wrong person, in the wrong place and makes a big fuss about secrets. Trying to protect a secret causes anxiety and discomfort. Love is seeing God in those next to us, Meditation is seeing God within us.

An ignorant one is not comfortable with a secret, whether revealed or unrevealed, but the wise one is comfortable with a secret whether revealed or unrevealed!

It is foolish to be perturbed by foolishness. Foolishness cannot overpower or annihilate wisdom nor does foolishness stay all the time. When you are not well-founded in wisdom, then foolishness perturbs you, throws you out of balance. When you create space for foolishness, you do not get perturbed by it, rather you will laugh and move on. Otherwise, you hate, get angry or become stressed by foolish acts.

When you know that truth is eternal and invincible you take foolishness as a joke and remain unmoved by it. Those who are averse to foolishness or get irritated by it are the members of the fools club.

Beware! Do not sign up.

First, anger is to be tamed. Know this: When the mind is so joyful and contented, when you are in meditation and leave room for imperfections and mistakes, you don't get angry in the first place. Know that no mistake can be corrected with anger. Only with awareness can anything be corrected.

Bliss comes out of chaos and the ability to enjoy chaos is enlightenment.

Valmikiji was one of the contemporaries of Sri Rama. Many scriptures in the world were written much after the physical presence of the Master, but Valmiki wrote the *Ramayana* in the very period when it happened. There was no division of castes in the society at that time. Honesty, human values and belongingness were so strongly rooted then.

You know, the world once was a beautiful place to live in where all would celebrate diversity. But what happened that caused so much division? I would want all to rise above the differences and move ahead. Whatever your attitude is from outside but have that naturalness from inside. Have the skill to create belongingness with all.

Do you all have cell phones? How does a cell phone work? First, it is to be fully charged. But if it is charged, but no sim card! So you need a sim card, and then you need to be in the range of the tower. When all three are there, the cell phone works. Similarly, for life to be successful three things are required: Seva, Satsang and Kripa (grace).

Know that you have abundance of grace with you, and God is your very own. Satsang is the charger and Seva is the sim card. What

happens with Seva? When you do Seva, you gain blessings and those blessings add strength to your life. And then Sadhana (Practices)? What is Sadhana? – That which makes you establish connection with the Self, with the Divine, that Infinite Power.

Just a conviction, I belong to Divine, whosoever is Divine! Divine principle is not someone in the sky. Inside you in the form of consciousness!

Every instant we are getting something to learn from the whole world. All that is needed is awareness!

Each individual is a beautiful Scripture designed by God. Study your own mind and then observe the minds of people around. What do we do? We don't observe our own minds but we keep on wasting efforts in judging others' minds. First, understand your own mind and then you will be able to understand what's happening in the big mind, in the minds of all.

You know, whomsoever I meet in the world, I feel that belongingness. I never feel I am meeting someone for the first time. So many times we have come to this world. I know a little bit, but you have forgotten. Keep smiling this time.

You can bring social transformation. The spirit needs to be strengthened. Your spirit is very ancient and pay some attention to that as well. Those who are devoid of spiritual knowledge are like undernourished people. Dividing in the list of priorities, the first priority is to strengthen one's very roots, having that sense of pride in one's very roots.

When you think good of yourself, you think ill of others, and when you think others are good, you think you are not OK. Such complexes are there in many children today. So the attitude that neither I am bad nor anybody else is bad gives such a sense of acceptance of everybody and your own self. Sadhana enables one deprogram

all past programming.

Meditation helps to change your perspective. It improves the way you perceive things. It brings clarity in the mind. It improves your interaction with people around –what you say, how you react and act in different situations, you become more aware. In general, from a stress-free society to peace and health in individuals and from a violence-free society to a sorrow-free soul – all are the side effects of meditation.

A profound Explanation to the Age of the Soul

Do you remember your age? Whatever it is 25-30 years! Where were you before these 25-30 years? Where would you be after 50-60 or say 100 years. Mumbai existed before you were born, this Ocean existed then too.

Do you remember how you entered your mother's womb?

Do you remember how you came out in this world?

Until the age of five the child remembers his/her past birth. The child recognizes colours or says certain things but elders tend to overlook that.

You know, this whole universe is a play of *prana*, the life-force. Everything here has some life-force. However, the units of *prana* differ;

Stone (Pathar) has 1 unit of *prana*

Water (Pani) has 2 units of *prana*

Fire (Agni) has 3 units of *prana*

Air (Hava) has 4 units of *prana*

Ether (Akash) has 5 units of *prana*

Animals and trees each have 6-7 units of *prana*

A human being has 8 units of *prana*. Hence he is called as *Ashtavasu*. But humans are born with a possibility to blossom into a fully blossomed state. Lord Krishna has the highest units of *prana* – 16. That is why He is referred to as a fully blossomed being.

You often see that every god/goddess travels on an animal. Goddess Durga riding on a tiger! It seems so imaginative. It doesn't click to the intellect, but this is so scientific. Each animal brings

certain cosmic vibrations on the planet. Example, the Peacock descends to the planet the vibrations of goddess Saraswati (The goddess of knowledge), the Bull's body radiation brings Shiva is Consciousness (The transformational and meditative aspect of nature). Right now all Devtas are here in this consciousness; all different energies are in this consciousness. All the mantras invite these auspicious vibrations.

Do you know the meanings of the months?

January, February... November, December. You all keep saying the months and you don't know the meanings!

September (Sapt+Ambar): 7th sky

November (Nav+Ambar): 9th sky

Do you know which languages these months belong to?

They are all derived from Sanskrit. Sanskrit was the only original language that was prevalent in the universe at the start.

February is referred to as 'Fag End'.

March means 'To Go Ahead'. Iraq, Iran, Kurdistan, everywhere they celebrate New Year in the month of March. In some less affected parts of India as well! So December (Dash+Ambar: 10th sky) makes the 10th sky.

You are older than the names of the months. Go deep in meditation to experience all this. Else keep it at the back of the mind that I am much older than my age. Sometime in life it will come to you.

Mind means moods, thoughts, opinions, ideas; all these things that we collect. And, no mind is meditation. Dawn and dusk are considered very good for meditation. So, whenever you meditate, or whenever the bad time is there, you meditate. When you meditate, you go off the influence of the mind and go into the self. The self is Shiva *tattva*. Shiva *tattva* means, always benevolent, caring, loving, uplifting. That consciousness deep within you which is caring, loving, uplifting and benevolent, will nullify the negative influences of the mind and the time.

As long as there is connection, there is attention – there is always

'give and take'. You will always receive blessings. You will always receive bliss and unwanted things will just drop off.

And it is nice of you to think that way – it also shows the level of consciousness. In this level of consciousness, drop this identity of garbage as part of you or yours. You find something pricking the mind, just see it as garbage, not yours or someone else's.

□

A Profound Explanation on the Power of Positive Thoughts and Words

In the pressure cooker, when you are cooking, when there is more pressure – how is it built up? Water vapour! And is that more powerful than water or not? So, the subtler you go, the more powerful the things are. Now, this thing (Guruji shows the small silver cymbals in the hands) has silver molecules. When you break the silver molecules down, you get into atomic particles, and, when you break him/her, you get sub-atomic molecules, which is minuter than the minutest. Are they not powerful? Which is powerful – this cymbal is powerful or the atom is powerful? Atom is powerful.

The subtler we go, it becomes more and more powerful. Though, everything is made up of consciousness. This entire universe is made up of consciousness, when you become subtler and subtler, they become more powerful.

Today I was watching a research done with water in Japan by a gentleman. He kept a little water in a bottle and took a photograph. Later he used the same water for prayer and then after prayer he took a photograph. You can see the impact of prayer – the subtle thought vibration has gone into the water. It's obviously visible.

He took a bottle of water and kept blaming it and then took a microscopic picture of it. With another bottle, he said some pleasing words and you can see the difference.

In India, this process is called *Abhimantra*. You take a pot of water, place your hand on top and then chant mantras. The mantras are supposed to be absorbed into the water. It is an old tradition in India. When you go to any holy man or saint, you take a pot of water and ask him to bless the water. Among the Sindhi community, they do this a lot.

This *Abhimantra* – mantra chanting on the water – has a huge impact on the water, because 70% of our body is water. In the Rudrabhisheka, water is made to fall on a crystal *lingam* while a particular chanting is being done and then it flows down. That water is very charged and it helps to uplift the atmosphere.

Now it is visible in the microscopic images, the changes that happen by these practices.

Similarly a gentleman from Russia came and conducted an experiment in Mahabalipuram, Tamil Nadu when they were doing the *Aarti*. He took the pictures and found that all the negative ions in the atmosphere suddenly disappeared; they turned into positive ions. It is the positive ions which bring changes. All these things are meant to create the positive ions; to bring the required changes. The same is the case with the use of fire. During fire ceremonies, when they put the mantra with the intention, there is a qualitative change that happens in the atmosphere.

When you want to take something from the world, the world will appear to be completely dull and lack. But when you want to contribute, the picture changes completely!

When you drop this wanting permanency, there will be peace.

Why do you want to explore hell now? I have never been there, so I can't tell you what it is.

When you don't want anything in return, that is called unconditional love. Not even a thank or a sense of gratitude or gratefulness. A lot of time people help others but these little expectations are there and that is what bugs him/her and pulls him/her down. That is also a condition.

Unconditional love comes naturally as your consciousness blossoms. You can't force it on yourself or cultivate it. I don't know how to cultivate it. It's simply a phenomenon. When your consciousness expands, rises, then, what comes out of it is unconditional love. You say, I'm here for you and I want nothing from you. This comes to you and it has come to you with some people but with many others, you have some expectations.

Just with a smile. In this world, there is place for ignorance as well. If someone is blaming you, it is out of his/her ignorance. And if it is not ignorance, it is mal-intention or jealousy and I would club all these emotions as part of ignorance. So, the best is you move on and don't get stuck because you have no way to control other's opinion and you don't need to – everyone can have his own opinion. The best formula is to educate and ignore. You have to; if someone says, you are a thief, you can't say, let him have his opinion. You educate him. If they believe it or not it's up to him/her. So, keep this as a formula in every relationship. Educate and ignore. If you just ignore in the beginning, you will only exhibit arrogance. 'Educate' is also a little strong word. You can say inform and ignore, which is even better. In education, there is more effort. In anger, people say, "I will teach him a lesson."

The person who has created chaos wants a cover and in the cover, he will always say to save his face and position. He will bring up many justifications. So, you understand that position – maybe you'd be doing the same thing when you are in that position. Don't depend on what people say. Most of our problems begin when we lock on to their words and not their feelings or where they stand. A mother says to the child, 'Get lost' and she doesn't really mean it but the words that come are very powerful and if the child takes on the words, then, he/she gets into trauma unnecessarily. I would say you should see beyond words.

Your communication should be more than verbal – it should transcend the verbal communication. Even if someone says all nasty things to you, can you just be grounded and keep your mind at calm, Then, you have achieved something. You are able to connect to people

beyond their words.

Don't expect that they should also connect. It's always one way. I tell you communication is always one-sided. You have the skill, you can communicate and you can receive it in that sense. You do not worry about what their reactions are, what they blabber.

They usually say all these blame games are blabbering and you get caught up in this blame game. Someone blames, you get caught up in this blame game. You stand up and say – "I have the master key and I know which button to press and how people will react and how things would change". You should have this confidence – the soul, the spirit in you is the master key. It can turn around the situation, the way you want it. You should have that faith. It may not happen five times but the sixth time it will happen. It all depends on your conviction and persistence. And don't bother about what they say.

The ways of karma are unfathomable. Karma is like an ocean. This is not one lifetime. In many lifetimes, we have done so many actions and they all have repercussions. Which karma has sprouted from which seed and what fruit this karma will give is very difficult to pinpoint. That is why it is said 'gahana karmanogati'. Unfathomable are the ways of karma. Because it is not just one lifetime, many lifetimes, we have done many things and we don't know which karma sprouts when. That's why don't worry about the karma, just be active and follow your conscience.

Act with conscience!

When you are taking responsibility, just take the responsibility. Doership means brooding over the consequences.

Whatever has happened, the moment you take responsibility, you are empowered. You come to the present. You have already accepted the consequences.

When you are in action, don't get into this philosophy of doership or non-doership, else the mind gets confused. When you act, you act a hundred per cent. When you are acting hundred per cent, suddenly you will realize I am not doing, it is all happening. Non-doership is an experience; it is not something you try to do or achieve.

The mind is like space. The self is like the space inside and outside the body. Thoughts come and go, emotions come and go but when you go inside, there is only empty space. When we identify ourselves with thoughts, feelings and emotions; that is when we feel we are stuck. The 'Real, Magnanimous You' are that space inside where you feel totally at peace. Those moments when you are totally in peace or fully in love, you feel an expansion, right? You feel boundless and limitless and that is our true nature. We are all one in that, there is no two!

If thoughts are coming, never mind, you know. When you realize, you again come back, observe the breath and just sit, that's it. Some irrelevant, absurd thoughts come and go, it's all part of stress release, hmm? You may get some brilliant thoughts or some very bad thoughts, don't judge at that time, we don't need to get excited, just relax. After meditation if you have some brilliant thoughts you may write him/her down, you may get some poems, some ideas, creativity may come. That's all fine, OK? So, just relax, hmm? Some people get ideas, some people can see some visions, some colours, some experience – some may smell some fragrance, or feel something – any of the 5 senses, I would say even the sixth sense, can just get activated during meditation, and it's good. With all the hollow and empty meditation what's happening is that the nervous system is getting clearer, purer and so it's reflecting the inner realm, hmm?

If you have to compare, you should compare with yourself – how you were yesterday, day before, two years back – that's healthy. Compare with yourself. See you've moved. You will always find you are moving when you compare with yourself, okay? Comparing with others, not about your personality, but in the work, is okay. If someone has done better, then you feel inspired to do better than they. It's okay. You don't have to keep your eyes shut. You know if you see

somebody has done better than you in business you put your target, so you do better than they. This is okay to do, that's what you should do. Comparison should inspire you, not put you down. First of all accept you don't know who you are, you have no idea who you are. You're not self-realized, remember this! If you have that feeling, "Oh, I'm so bad, I'm like this, I'm like…" you have no idea who you are. You have infinite potential inside you. You can do ten times better than anybody else, better than what you're doing right now, hmm? So Comparison should only inspire you, not pull you down. If you think you know about yourself, and you feel you are weak and think you don't have ability then it pulls you down but when you know there's infinite potential inside you, you don't know who you are, then the comparison will only inspire you to do better work.

You know, take good sleep. You don't have to wake up at 4 o'clock and do practice, no. You do it when you're complete with your sleep. Whenever you have complete sleep and you wake up, then you do it, okay? Don't strain yourself. Our rule is what? Not to torture yourself or strain yourself, hmm? Your inner connection can only happen when you are relaxed, not if you're tense.

Liberation simply means freedom. Then you can say, 'I want nothing for myself, I'm complete.' Liberation is when you have accepted the whole creation the way it is; you've accepted people the way they are. Liberation is total peace; a peace which is unshakeable. And this sort of peace dawns when there is forgiveness, compassion, naturalness. You know if you assume you're somebody then you can't, if you are intelligent or stupid you have no liberation. You are neither intelligent nor stupid, neither rich, nor poor – if you think – 'Oh, I'm a very poor guy or poor lady,' no way you can get it! I am nothing! That sense of lightness, easiness, is what liberation is. A simple taste of it everyone has got, you know when? When your exams were over! The day you finished your exams when you were a child you came back home and threw those books on the sofa and just sat, relaxed! How did it feel? Great, huh? That's all!

When you achieve success, if that is your goal – to achieve your dream – you should be ready to face some obstacles on the path. And you know that every obstacle is only bringing out more skills out of you, it will not deter you from your goal but will only bring in whatever is needed to fulfil your dream. Do you get what I'm saying? The obstacles that come on the path are only to bring in more skills and they won't deter or de-track you from your goal.

Take longer time to eat…longer time. You know, usually people who overeat, they eat so fast. They stuff things so fast, but if you keep the food in your mouth, chew it longer, just feel the food in your mouth, you will see you can consume only half of what you usually consume, yes.

In work, don't use your emotions – in work use your intellect. But with your family and friends don't use your intellect so much, use your emotions. If you mix it up, you are in trouble! You know, with your wife and children if you are relating him/her with your intellect and doing business with your emotion, you had it! You know at home you have to be more with the value of heart. When you do service, you do it with your heart, right? But when you're doing your work you don't have to be an emotional thing. Just use your rational mind.

A Profound Explanation on Marriage

In a marriage you should consider the other person as your own part, part – like your arm, like your body. It's two bodies, one mind, one soul. So, whatever your spouse desires, you make it your own desire, that's it. Your spouse's taste, consider it as your own taste. See, you have many different tastes, right? Sometimes you like this, sometimes you like that. When do the conflict arise? When your tastes

start moving apart. You should start saying your taste is my taste; your pleasure is my pleasure. I am here for you, rather than, what can you do for me? When we start 'What can you do for me?' then both become unhappy, yes? But when you say, 'What can I do for you? I'm here for you.' This is the only mantra. Happy marriages are what? 'I'm here for you, come what may, happy times or unhappy times!' See in life sometimes there are disappointments, sometimes there is success. In either case, 'I'm with you.' This is one thing. The second thing is, if one is upset, the other should not get upset at the same time. Choose a different time to get upset. Know that 'Oh, my spouse is upset! Okay.' Give him or her the time to be upset. Don't question 'Why are you so upset?'If someone is upset, the other gets angry and expects him/her not to be upset. This is a big mistake! Someone is upset, leave him/her that space. You know many of us don't even know how to receive love! See, someone comes and keeps telling you, 'Oh, I love you, I love you so much, I love you!!!' Suddenly you go, 'Wow, what do I say now!? How do I react?' You get into a corner; you don't know how to react. You don't know what to say, so that person who kept saying, 'I love you, I love you, I love you!!!', suddenly finds you are not responding, then starts accusing you, 'See, look, you're so cold!' 'See you don't know how to love. You never said you love me!' and blah, blah, blah… Demand – Demand destroys love. Never demand love from your spouse. Take it for granted that he/she loves you, but that's it, finished, you know! So when one starts demanding and policing one's spouse, one gets into a mess, right!

Be like a child, unassuming, knowing the more you know there is so much more to be known. Knowing only leads to awareness that you do not know so much more. That brings humility. Do you see what I'm saying?

For God's sake don't do anything with your ego! Just let it be. If you find you have a big ego, don't try to get it out of yourself. Let it be. You know, trying to meddle with your ego becomes a bigger

problem. Then you say, 'Look, I erased my ego!' 'Nobody could do this!' Understand that? You know it's so difficult to get rid of the ego. It's like saying – 'I'm the most humble person in the world! You can't find anyone with more humility than I!' Does it make any sense? So if you find there is any ego, let it be like that happily, huh? Don't try to meddle or get rid of it. Just smile, yes! You know ego is stiffness. When you're at home, you relax. When you feel ease, then ego is not there. The antidote for ego is just being natural. Or one day if you want to act crazy or foolish, it might help you a little bit, because your greatest fear is what others will think. Give everyone freedom to think whatever they want to think, right? Then you'll find you're so much at ease, at peace with yourself.

The balloon has air outside and inside it. Inside a vessel, there is space and outside there is space as well. The inside space is jeeva, the outside space is Brahma. The jeeva is desire, aversion, craving. All this is the balloon. That is why the Lord is not somebody separate, but it is, 'What I am.' If the wave asks, 'Where is the ocean?' Then what to say? The wave itself is the ocean. You have to only realize this. That is why it is said that while it takes a moment to break a flower stem, the Divine can be realized in a fraction of that moment.

Tell everybody to be friends with animals. Once you are friends, you don't eat him/her. Like you don't use your pets as food. Once you have cultivated a relationship, you do not eat it. Cultivate the habit of befriending all the species and this is the way of turning the world, vegetarian.

When desires arise just see whether it is beneficial for you or not. When desires come up and pass through the intellect, then it is good. If it is just an unqualified desire, it could cause problems.

To get over habits, there are three options. If someone tempts

you: Suppose you stop this bad habit for 10 days you will get 10 lakh rupees. Then you will do it. Something higher than your habit can create greed in you. Or if someone creates fear in you: Example, a doctor says if you drink, you will spoil your liver. Then you can get over your habit. The third way is through love.

People are bad because there is some stress. Once they have got onto the path of sadhana, they can come out of it.

What does wealth mean? Not just money, whatever supports life is wealth. In Scandinavia, people thirst for the sun. When I had gone there in winter, it was dark like it's here now. When I asked someone, 'When will the sun rise?' They said, 'In January.' That is wealth for him/her.

Today there is a need for a spiritual wave in society. A Spiritual wave just means where people feel connected to one another. When belongingness increases, corruption decreases.

There are different types of Samadhi.

1. Laya Samadhi – Just listening to music you dive deep
2. Sakshi Samadhi – Mindful awareness

If you do too much, that also is not good. That is why one should sit with a teacher and take guidance.

When somebody leaves the body we realize the magnitude of life. A person, who was there, is no more. It brings a depth to life. One starts wondering – what is life? Where did the person go? It gives a depth to life, there is no point in brooding. Yes, tears come, you don't need to suppress it. But there is no need to brood over it.

In the Bhagavad Gita, Lord Krishna talks about all the good qualities. And then He adds that they are already in you. Negative qualities have come because of company, etc. You don't need to get

positive qualities. Just like in an atom, the core is positive and the negativity is peripheral, If you feel that deep inside you is sorrow or anger then you can never get rid of it. Don't ever think deep inside you is sorrow or anger. Modern psychology sometimes says this sorrow is deep inside you. It's wrong. They know nothing about consciousness. Negativity is not skin-deep. Know that it's not in the core.

Lord Krishna says to Arjuna, 'Whatever you are seeing in this world, that is all a little part of Me. Wherever you see any merit, that comes from Me only. Any intelligence that you see in anyone, that is Me only. Any valour that you see in anyone, that is Me only. The whole world reflects in a little part of Me.'

How do you ride a bicycle? Do you allow yourself to fall on one side? When you are more towards one side, you just balance. But one strong conviction should be there – I will do seva, I will do studies, I will take care of my family and respect the elders as well. These are not opposites but complementary. When you do seva, you get power and achieve merit, and that gives you good fortune. So, spirituality brings strength. Through meditation, you will progress in the world.

This conviction, 'I will be able to do all', works miracles.

If you find any doubt, just know that it is temporary. The most important thing is to develop a strong personality. Going to college, stuffing your head with information and just passing the exam, no! How much strength and humility have you gained? Are you blossoming into a complete person? It is important to check this. Enthusiasm with awareness! Seva brings out the skill in you that will again make a difference in how you relate to all types of people. Softness and depth will come to you. With enthusiasm, there will be awareness. All can be threaded on a string.

To be innocent, drop cunningness. Innocence is naturally present

in everyone. You just need to blossom it. And how do you do that? Just be in meditation. 'I am nothing – Akinchan, I don't want anything, and all are my very own; I accept all and all accept me.' When you know that everybody is accepting you, you move ahead with naturalness. When you think people are not accepting you the way you are, then you think of doing something to gain acceptance and you start becoming unnatural.

When you get something after asking, your faith gets developed. And then even without asking you get what you need.

To get into your train, you need to put effort, you take your luggage and go to the right platform. But once you are on the train, you put your luggage aside and relax.

You keep putting your effort. There is a proverb, 'Try and try again and at last you will succeed.' So, perhaps you don't succeed the first time or second time. Yet if your intention is strong, it will happen.

Just assume that it is there. Don't put effort. Surrender is there – simply assume this and move on.

Don't think those who eat non-vegetarian food are sinful. It is only that tamasic tendencies are encouraged when one eats non-vegetarian food. That won't be good for him/her, for the world and for society. My dear, don't make your stomach a graveyard.

Faith and knowledge are co-related. Because when there is knowledge, there is faith. And where there is faith, there is knowledge. So you have faith and that is why you are asking. You have faith that I will answer it and you will take my answer. So, knowledge and faith are all connected.

A part of destiny is fixed, and certain things can change.

If you look at the benefits that meditation brings in our life, you will find that it is all the more relevant. In ancient times, meditation was used as a way for finding the Self, for enlightenment. Meditation was a way to overcome misery and problems. It's the way to develop one's abilities.

If you want, keep aside enlightenment. Today's stress and tension in society calls for meditation. If you take more responsibility, more meditation is required. The greater responsibilities and ambitions you have, the greater is the need for you to meditate. If you have nothing to do, you may not need meditation as much.

The busier you are, the lesser time you have, the more desires and ambitions you have – all the more is the need to meditate. Because meditation not only relieves you of stress and strain, it also enhances your abilities, strengthens your nervous system and mind. Not only does it help eliminate stress and tensions, releasing toxins from the body and soothing the mind, but also makes you more capable, enhances you in every way. What else do you want?

I would say if you want to be happy and healthy, you've got to meditate.

From thousands of years people have passed this technical knowledge. Usually, most Masters will test a student before even teaching meditation. They would give this knowledge only to someone who qualifies. They would wait for the right student to come to impart this knowledge. In the past, it used to be very tough, you had to please the Master before you could get anything from Him.

I took a very different stance, I opened the flood gates, gave it to everyone, let everybody progress as per one's sincerity and capability.

You can't be a surgeon for yourself. You may be a surgeon but you can't be your own surgeon, right? So your mother is your first

Guru. A mother teaches you. Of course, a Guru is one who is unconditional in his attitude and approach towards you. You should play a role of a Guru unconditionally. You help others or care for someone with wisdom. Then you are playing the role of a Guru to him/her too.

If you help somebody with an attitude of 'I want nothing, I just want your progress', then you're a Guru to him/her. Yet don't demand him/her to accept you as Guru. No, a real Guru does not demand anything, not even gratitude from somebody.

Corruption is at three levels. One is among people. People often accept corruption as a way of life. Second the bureaucracy; and third, the politicians. There are good people in every stratum of life. And there are not so good people. We should bring him/her to The Art of Living course and teach him/her the breathing techniques. They'll become better.

The root cause of violence is stress and anger. And the only way I know to reduce stress and anger is through meditation, pranyama, Sudarshan Kriya. This is the only way. You can do something with ayurveda, can change the diet… you can do those things, yet they are all secondary.

You know, knowledge and logic, and music are formed in two different parts of our brain and they're both essential. That brings a balance in the system. Music is essential.

All possible...It's possible to know him/her if they incarnate now and you can feel that? Haven't you felt that you go somewhere and suddenly you feel someone is very close to somebody? Your gut feeling comes. It's all possible. You know, we're all connected in some time or another. In the past, we've all been connected. Now we are connected. Whether we acknowledge or not, we are all connected.

When you say, 'I want nothing'. That is happiness. When you are happy and are asked: 'Do you want anything?' you say 'No, I want nothing.'

How does one deal with self-doubt? Understand doubt: doubt is always about something that is good. Someone tells you 'I love you', you ask him/her 'Really?', and they say 'I hate you', you never ask 'Really?' So, a doubt is always about something good. You doubt your abilities; you never doubt your weaknesses. You doubt happiness, you never doubt misery, isn't it? Nobody doubts their depression. 'But well, I'm not sure if I'm happy or not, well I'm not sure'. So when you understand that the doubt is always about something that's positive, your mind shifts to a level, a different level altogether.

Doubt is simply low prana. If you do more pranayamas you will see that you have come above that.

Now don't try hard to become a devotee. Love combined with commitment is devotion. Love with wisdom is devotion.

Love without wisdom can turn into negativities: Love today, hate tomorrow. Love today, jealousy tomorrow. Love today, possessiveness tomorrow.

Love combined with wisdom is bliss, and that is devotion. Devotion is a strong bond, a sense of belongingness. Everybody is born with it. It's just like becoming a child again.

You don't have to learn anything from illness. Just move on. It's part of life. The body undergoes some illnesses. It could be many reasons. It could be due to karma, to past impressions, to the genes in the family. It could be due to violating laws of Nature, eating too much when you should not eat, and it could be due to all this technology that we are having around which causes so much radiation. So it doesn't pay us sitting and analyzing what I should learn from this.

Just keep moving with one faith, one knowledge, one sense of gratefulness. We are happy we are on this planet, as long as we are here, let's do good. One day, we'll all be gone. For sure, we'll all be gone.

Life is a balance between these two things. Taking responsibility and letting go. It's both. That's a fine balance. For the present and the future, take responsibility, for the past know that it has to happen that way and move on. So often we do the reverse. We think that the past was free will and regret and we think the future is all destiny and we don't do anything about it. But the wise one does you know what? He regards the future as free will, the past as destiny and he is happy in the present. So you don't regret about the past and you know what you want to do in the future; and you are on it.

Anand Tandav – Meditating while being merged in the dance of creation! Shiva consciousness means that which is pure and complete. When both the shores of sound and silence, music and meditation are inculcated in life then only perfection dawns! We will meditate for some time now! There are three rules to meditation – For some time, I do nothing, I want nothing and I am nothing. Whatever you need, think of that afterwards. I am neither intelligent nor stupid, I am neither rich nor poor, I am neither sinful nor a noble soul – Akinchan, Achah and Aprayatan!

Yoga is the art of doing nothing. Being in a total calm and serene state of mind is yoga, and yoga enables one to reach such a state of mind. Physical yoga is to reduce tamoguna. A little practice of being peaceful before and after doing work gives such strength and erases so many distortions from the mind. More are the distortions, the more sorrow one experiences.

Is there any profit of being angry at the past? A business-minded person would never do that!

There is a story of Mullah Nassurudin. His son was about to

hold an expensive electronic equipment and he slapped his son. When asked, he said what the fun would be to slap after it had broken! It is a sign of foolishness to be angry at something that had happened in the past. People ask me if I don't get angry. But at what should I be angry at? Past that has already gone!

You get angry at something which is happening in the present. But reacting to anger with anger! What foolishness! If somebody does a mistake again and again, you can show anger but don't get swayed away with that. Arogya vardhak gussa – Healthy anger is that which stays only for that much time as a line drawn on water stays.

It doesn't mean not to show anger when someone is wrong but it is unintelligent to flow away with that. Sadhana is to protect mind from any vikara (distortion that takes one away from the self).

Nature may put many vikalpa on the way to shake your faith. Satsang, the right company, would help. Which is the right company? That which makes you feel light, which makes you feel the problem is very trivial as compared to what you thought. That is no satsang which makes you perceive an exaggerated view of the problem.

Nature may put 1000 hurdles on the way but you come out smilingly with a much strong personality. This is just another way of Nature to strengthen the faith. An enormous strength rises in you. Your faith in God is no favour to God! One who has tasted the devotion, He knows. Sankalpa gets manifested with devotion. When your devotion is strongly rooted, Nature listens to you!

Happiness comes by grace, joy comes by grace, and even devotion comes by grace. Whatever one gets in life that comes with grace. Every instant one is grateful to the God being beneficial for one self and for others as well!

Live your life which radiates a fragrance which makes you and also others happy.

These cell phones are so powerful that you can reach anybody in the world through him/her. So, the mind which has made these cell phones, won't that be more powerful than these things? If these radiations can produce such effect, what effect would human radiations produce?

The sankalpa that one takes for the goodness of society that definitely gets accomplished. Drop your worries and the Divine will care of you. Be in the innocent state of surrender.

Don't make an effort. It takes its natural course. Never try to hold on to joy, happiness and inspiration. When you try to, it runs even more quickly.

Before Quantum Physics came into the picture and ancient Vedic knowledge was revived, a lot many were into linear thinking. According to linear thinking, there is beginning to everything and everything comes to an end. But we were of spherical thinking – No beginning and no end. The adwait (Non-dual) existence!

Everything here radiates vibrations, and those vibrations make things happen around you.

The first and foremost identity is that you are a part of Divine. You are a beautiful human being. Then you can be a Hindu, a Muslim, a Christian, an Engineer, a Teacher or whatever. All identities come later.

In life, there should be all types of prosperity – usually money is associated with prosperity. Satisfaction is true wealth. The air, earth and time are also wealth. The right usage of time is very important. There is a wealth in knowledge. Its nectar should be in our consciousness. Whatever we have, whatever we can give, should be shared. We must practise charity.

The more happiness we share with others, the more happiness we experience. Do you agree with it? Don't just say 'yes'. First, you think and if you agree, then accept that. One can travel the whole world, but only in the Indian tradition you will see that even when the best of knowledge is spoken, one says, 'You think about it, only if you find it's right, then accept it.'

After reciting 18 chapters of The Bhagvad Gita, Lord Krishna tells Arjuna, 'You think about it, analyze it, if it appeals to your mind and if you agree then you accept it.' This means the strength that is within us; the strength of the soul is what gives us this freedom. So now we have to utilize it in the right direction. So whenever we are happy and joyful, we should make an effort to spread this happiness, this joy to minimum ten other people. Will you all do it? Everybody? In my opinion, each person has the capability to give happiness to a thousand people. Each one of you can bring light to the lives of a thousand people or more.

Like I said, spirituality is the only way through which we can be free from depression. Whether our society gets freedom from misconduct, corruption, injustice or not, we must spread spirituality. In every house, we must tell people to meditate, to get together and have satsang. In whichever village, people have got together and done satsang, all negativities have gone away. Mahatma Gandhi had once desired for an honest society that is now becoming a reality in many villages in India. Even in Gujarat, in many villages, this work is going on where people have left alcohol and drugs. With much joy and love they are serving others.

One thing that is very important for you to remember – In everyday life, you may experience some laxity here and there. Your mind gets upset or someone has tears in his eyes... this is all part of life, which keeps happening. It has never been like everything in

life is perfect, ideal or rosy-rosy. It has never been like that, but to deal with problems we need strength and patience and that comes through sadhana. Don't think of life as separate from sadhana, your life itself is your sadhana. Understand this and move forward.

Don't think that just by closing my eyes for a few minutes and doing something, sadhana is done. No! Whatever you do, walking, moving about, getting up or sitting down, smiling or getting angry, whatever you do in life is sadhana. We need to look from this perspective and then we experience so much relief. When in yourself, this cool breeze of relief and peace starts to flow then you will see how people around you will also start to feel the same. Many people are already feeling it, isn't it?

It is said that devotion was born in Tamil Nadu, raised in Karnataka and blossomed in Gujarat. So here in Gujarat, devotion blossomed and became complete. Where is the blossoming of devotion? It is in service! We must do as much seva as we can. This does not mean we have to do what we cannot do. No. We have to do as much as is possible for us; and there is nothing as big or small service, the fruit of all service is the same. We must not feel that I have to do that service which is important or big, no; what is important is to have the feeling to be of help to others, and we serve with that feeling. It is in your nature to help and you are helping by doing that. That's it!

If any of you are feeling 'I am doing a lot of seva', remove that from your mind today. Who are you doing seva for? Without doing something we cannot live. That's why we are doing something and if others are benefiting by us doing something, then it is a very good thing, isn't it. So we must not feel proud of our seva or proud of our good qualities, this is what we need to offer into the fire of knowledge. So offer your negative qualities, also offer your good qualities and good actions, and live life smiling, feeling light and at the same time being immersed into the depths of knowledge.

You don't have to work very hard to achieve love and peace in your life; this is easily achieved in a state of rest and such rest we can experience when there are no small botherations lingering in the mind. Then you experience deep rest; and desires linger in your mind when you do not have faith. When you are thirsty then only the desire for water arises, but what will happen if you sit and think about water all day? Do you understand what I am saying? What does desire mean? A lack of faith that I am going to get what I need. So with satsang, sadhana and seva, our faith becomes very strong and all work gets done like it's getting done in your lives right now.

How many of you have experienced that what you desire is getting fulfilled? So whatever you desire is getting fulfilled, then you should desire for big things. What is the use of desiring for small things? There is no fun in that.

I am not saying do this, do that, I am saying do nothing. Now just five minutes before I said spread happiness, now I am saying you don't have to do anything. Just relax… the contradiction between these two states only is life. That's why if you read the Gita you will understand everything is contradictory. The Gita is our very life; it is not only a holy text. The Gita is for everybody, it is our life and in life, there are contradictions.

You give your 100 per cent, do whatever you can, and then if somebody expects more, it is their problem.

As your mind blossoms, new aspects of the knowledge will blossom in you. Knowledge is structured in consciousness.

Understanding Chapter 7 of the Bhagwad Gita

When a yogi sleeps, everybody is awake. And when everyone is sleeping, a yogi is awake. This is what Lord Krishna says in the

Gita. You have already heard this. What does it mean? It simply means, when everyone is excited and worried, the yogi sleeps comfortably. The yogi knows that everything will happen for the best, and all happenings will be for the general good. A yogi has this confidence.

And when everyone else is sleeping, then the yogi is awake, meaning that the yogi is aware of the Truth about life when everyone is asleep, sleeping about the truth of life. Nobody wonders, 'What is going to be my end? Where will I go, what is life, who am I?' When none of these questions arise in people's mind, they are asleep.

People are lost in watching movies and playing video games. There are people who begin playing video games even at a very old age. Man is not seeing that death is coming near… He does not think, 'How I have filled my mind with so much craving and aversion. And I have done nothing to wash and cleanse my mind'. If you don't cleanse the mind of impressions, then you have to carry the same mind and same impressions with you even after death.

So when you die, your mind should be happy and joyful! One who is sleeping, he is taking all garbage into his mind. The yogi is alert and awake. He does not take any garbage from anybody into his mind: Why did this man say this to me? That lady says that to me?

Your mind is completely destroyed thinking about others' imperfections. Leave others' imperfections to others. Let him/her handle that. You handle your mind, you handle your imperfections, that is good enough. Do you have patience to accept others' mistakes? You have to accept others' mistakes? Correct him/her as much as you can. If you are so compassionate, only then you should correct it. Otherwise, leave it to Nature, they will find their own way. But if you are so compassionate, correct it with compassion, and then, it doesn't get into your head, your mind.

When do you get angry or upset? When you see someone else's action as imperfect. Can you correct somebody's action like this? His action is imperfect but now by thinking about it, your mind has become imperfect. At least, save your mind. Others have gone on the wrong path, why should you let your mind also dwell on the

wrong! Right? That is why He says, 'The yogi is awake when others are sleeping. When you are sleeping, you let others' garbage enter your mind. But yogis don't let this happen. They keep their mind fresh.'

Where does your mind go? It goes towards beauty, light, strength... Lord Krishna says, 'Wherever your mind goes, see me in that. If something is beautiful, it is because it has life in it. It is the same consciousness. So the mind goes back to the source.' Lord Krishna says: The light in the sun is Me. I am the liquid in water.

'I am the smell in the earth. I am the fire in fire.'

We are made up of the same substance as the sun. If there is no sun, there is no earth. If there is no earth, you too will not be there.

If you talk to a quantum physicist today, he will say the same thing – everything is made up of one wave function.

The same thing Lord Krishna said: 'I am the life in everybody.'

Turn our mind inward and look at the life force that we are.

In life, it is Me.

Life is God. God is not something outside the life. Life is Divine.

The life in this body is Divine. What is the mind craving for? This pleasure, that pleasure. Right now, attend to life. It is not that only my life is God. Life everywhere is the same Atma.

The seventh chapter is very beautiful.

In the Bhagwad Gita, the chapters unfold, step by step.

In the chapter on Vishad Yoga, Lord Arjuna is feeling so nervous, is trembling.

In Sakhya Yoga, Lord Krishna tells Arjuna, 'Awaken! Nothing has happened to your Atma. Happiness and sadness have come and go.'

In Karma yoga, Lord Krishna says: 'Act! You cannot do anything without action. Even you want to stand and sit, action is required. So, do something.'

After Karma yoga, its Gyan yoga: 'Understand what you're doing.'

After Gyan and karma, its Dhyan, where Lord Krishna says: 'Before acting, meditate. After finishing work, meditate.'

In that manner, the chapters unfold, step by step.

Look at the present moment – now, now, now! Wake up NOW! Everything else is stupid. All that has happened has gone into emptiness. Everything dissolves into emptiness. Your entire past – wiped out! All the things that you felt are gone. Good or bad, they are gone. So, wake up to the truth of the present moment. Divinity is in the present moment. This is yoga. Yoga is being established in the moment.

The sun rises in the east. So, in the morning, you meditate facing the east. But in the evening, you face the west because the sun sets in the west. Energy flows from where the sun is. So, when you face the sun, you are balanced. For prayer and meditation, you need balance – balance of mind, posture… See, it does not matter which direction you face when you meditate, as long as you are facing a direction and meditating.

□

Why did God Create So Many Galaxies, Universes, People? What was His Purpose?

Well, he couldn't find a better job to do!

It's obvious – you ask someone who is playing soccer. When so many people are fighting over that little ball, if an alien comes and watches 22 people fighting over one ball, he will ask, 'This world has so many things, why don't you just give a ball to each player? They are busy falling one another and kicking that one ball into the net, and so many people are happy about this. Why cause such a commotion? Just give him/her a ball and let him/her put it through the net.'

For an alien, this appears unintelligent and purposeless. But fans of soccer will say, 'Oh! we had such a fantastic time!' The one purpose of everything that man created is happiness. It is for the same purpose that God created all this. And He is enjoying it like He is watching a soccer game. No other purpose.

Love can resolve all relationships. See, it does not matter that people think you are a donkey. It does not matter! Just don't kick him/her and prove him/her right! From your side, be pleasant. Expecting nothing from anyone is the way to be happy. When we start expecting, we become miserable.

When you are sad or miserable, have the strength to sacrifice the cause of sadness. All you can pray is, 'When I am happy, let me do seva; when I am sad, let me have the strength to renounce.'

A lady once asked, 'Why did God make this place so sad?' So that you may turn to Him. Even though the world is so sad, you still cannot drop it! Can you imagine what would happen if it was all good? You have to turn to the Creator through the creation, recognize the Creator inside the creation. It's like a hologram.

During the moments of misery, we need the strength of sacrifice. During the moments of happiness, we need to share our happiness.

Pay someone to be after you when you are lazy. Tell him/her, 'If I am lazy, don't let me sit and lie down. Come get me with a stick.' Laziness goes away when you have a buddy who is after you.

There are three ways to get over laziness:

One, greed. If you are greedy for something, it will take you out of laziness. If someone tells you, 'If you do this pranayama for 40 days, you will get $1 million.' You will say, 'I will do for 45 days, just to be sure!'

Two, fear. Fear makes people fall into hoaxes. Some hoaxes even claim to cleanse Karmas. Karmas go away when you meditate. When you are in love, and serve, Karmas are erased. It is unfortunate that people don't know anything about spirituality – they have neither the experience nor have they read scriptures. This is where the Vedic tradition is important. So many seers laid down the rules. And then authenticated him/her to make sure they are not an illusion. But people still go into hoaxes, because of fear.

Three, love. When you are deeply in love, where is the question of laziness?

The fact that you are a sane human being is enough and the fact that you are a good human being. And all human beings are good!

Unfortunately, some scientists claim that human beings have dark and light sides. So the concept is that half of you is dark and half of you is light. That is not how it is. Just imagine someone coming up to you and saying, 'You have a dark side. You could be a murderer.' You would say, 'No, I didn't even dream of something like that!' Then you start wondering, 'Oh, maybe there is something like that inside me...' Then you put that seed in yourself and start nurturing that which was not there before.

There is a beautiful verse by the Indian poet Kabir, 'I went to find a bad person in the universe, and I found none.' There are negative tendencies in people but that is not the basic human nature. That is only on the circumference. Why is someone behaving negatively? Because he is hurt. A happy, joyful, centered person will never do harm to anyone, even to animals. See, even lions go for prey only when they are hungry, not all the time. That too, they don't kill other animals out of rage. They do it out of need.

So, these concepts that a person has a light and dark side are man-made, far from reality! Go into the soul, 'Satchidananda' – true, blissful: The Consciousness.

See, to catch a train, you have to hurry up, pack your things, go to the train station and get onto the train or go to the airport and catch a plane. But once you are on the plane, relax. Running between aisles holding your luggage will not get you to your destination any faster! Once you are on the path, relax.

Lord Krishna tells Arjuna after he has told him all that Arjuna had to do, 'Drop all that, I will relieve you from your sins. You drop all that you are holding onto. Drop even your dharma. I will relieve you from your sins.' Instead, people try to get rid of their sins. That will never happen. The Divine will relieve you of your sins.

All that you need to do is to let go of everything you are holding on to. It is beautiful. First, Lord Krishna makes Arjuna understand Dharma. Then, Arjuna is made to drop all of it. Lord Krishna says, 'Take refuge in Me and Me alone. I will relieve you of all your sins.'

Just be natural. For God's sake, relax. Don't practise awareness all the time. Awareness is essential, but don't practise it. Even the Gita says no extremities. Just relax.

Imagine listening to music being completely aware. No, music is to be enjoyed in relaxation. Doing is always limited. This applies to anything you do, including meditation. That is why meditation is something that must be allowed to just the way you want happen.

All the techniques create a situation for the mind to experience and go beyond its limitation. Even music creates an atmosphere to boost consciousness. Music is 'Laya Yoga'. Laya is dissolving. This is the highest form of Samadhi (unity with the Divine) that should also happen.

Bring a balance between awareness and this dissolution.

Hinduism is a way of life, and it has been around for millions of years. So many practices are just interpolations or add-ons. Imagine that in the winter you have a coat. You come into the house and hang up the coat before entering the house. This then becomes a practice and a rule comes that you can enter the house even in the summer only if you have a coat to hang up. The same applies here. Animal sacrifices have no scriptural sanction. The same thing is true for tongue piercing. Even Lord Krishna says that only a fool would torture his own body.

When knowledge lodges itself firmly in your heart, then it is wisdom.

The desire for Self-Realization is the highest desire, the only one worth pursuing. Whether you acknowledge this or not, everyone has come to this planet with this desire. If you have recognized this, it's very good.

Who is God according to you? Somebody sitting up in heaven! No! God is that from which nothing can escape. When the mind is totally relaxed, it merges in the Divine, it relaxes in the Divine. The whole point is to relax the mind in that soothing consciousness. When the wave is on the surface, it is a wave. But when it identifies itself with the depth of the ocean, it becomes the ocean.

God is love and it is inside each one of us.

Fear is love, upside down!

Love! That is what you are!

Longing is a prelude to love!

You can say that every loss is a prelude to a bigger gain.

To understand faith, you must know doubt.

Grace comes with gratitude. If you feel grateful, then something comes up in your life – and that is grace.

There is a science behind the sound of Omkar. Scientists have found that the frequency of the earth rotating around its axis is the same as that of OM. The graph plotted for the two frequencies is the same. So, whenever we chant OM, our vibes match with that of the earth's natural frequency, the natural law.

You have a mind and the mind passes through time. Why don't you observe it! You have different moods in the morning, different moods in the afternoon, and different moods in the evening and night, isn't so?

There is alertness and wakefulness at sunrise. I don't think anybody likes to listen to romantic songs at dawn, dusk or afternoon. Unless you are newly married or just fallen in love!

In the morning, the mind is in a state of knowledge, alertness and wakefulness.

It is action-oriented in the afternoon and in the evening, the mind is in a state of relaxation.

One who wants to be unhappy can be unhappy the whole time, and one who wants to be happy can be happy throughout the day. A fool will be unhappy all the time and the intelligent one will be happy in spite of changing moods. In the same way, seasons also affect the mind.

Definitely, the mind and time have a very unique relationship. If you have transcended the mind, there is happiness throughout. An eternal calmness and serenity dawns.

Deepening your roots means getting well grounded. That's it. It is not about any particular religion or culture. Deepen your roots means – be grounded and stable.

It is all right to make a mistake. Making a mistake is a part and parcel of life. Sometimes a mistake happens; it happens. Fine! Accept it and move ahead. The pain of making the same mistake again and again itself is good enough to take you out of the same mistake. The pain and pinch of suffering will make you come out of that. But never justify your mistake.

Don't recognize complexity. Keep your sight on the one. In Sanskrit it is said, 'Antarmukhi sada sukhi'. If your mind is turned inwards, it will always be happy. What is complex? People's mind! They are bothered about their complexity, why should you be bothered about the same? People are complex, and they will come down. Have patience and compassion.

There is a remedy to all celestial phenomena! You know what? 'Om Namah Shivaya'. The vibrations of the mantra create an armour around us and protect and energize the whole body – mind complex.

Rise in love! In love, you don't expect anything in return. If you want something in return, don't call it love. Then that's need. In a relationship, there is a need, but there is no need in love. Love is your very nature. If it sounds too philosophical for now, just keep it in the background and relax. One day you will understand, when your heart breaks or when you realize you expected something too much, something will pop up from the background of the mind and try to save you.

Suppose there is only a hero in a film and there is no villain! When there are all kinds of thrill, only then the movie works. If it would have been just a hero or heroine, they get married and live together, that's it! How would the film be? This is all a play, a drama. So, all kinds of things keep happening.

The soul is eternal. This world is ever changing, different changes keep on happening. Knowing this, just relax. Be of service. Wherever there is a need, be ready to jump in that. Service is our very nature and we cannot live without it. Service should not be like a heavy weight, but just like a flower petal – easy and natural.

Tragedy is tragedy when you are affected. There is no explanation for some phenomenon. Why do accidents happen, why do people die? It is these moments when you say 'Why me?' You know, the 'Why' in the mind is associated with misery and the 'How' is associated with wonder and joy.

When the question, 'Why is this problem only with me?' arises in mind or it arises in some other's mind, better don't say anything. Just be! No explanation, no reasoning of that will suffice. You simply have to leave those questions for those moments. Time will take you

across. Time will make you sail from that situation. Our tendency is to answer him/her or console him/her, but smile or a moment of silence will be better. No explanation. No reasoning, no theories will ever do anything. That is what I feel.

Ear piercing appears to be scientific, because all the nerves that create awareness in the brain end in the ear lobe. So, ancient people used to do so to create more attention.

What I have heard is:
Before marriage: a couple is mad for each other.
During marriage: They are made for each other.
And then: They are mad at each other.
After while: They are mad because of each other.
Somebody has formulated this!

One thing I know, marriage is an institution of patience, sacrifice, caring for each other and sharing. If one is upset, other should keep quiet and wait for his/her turn to get upset. If both together get upset at the same time, then there is a problem! But in front of kids, one should better be civilized.

Who says human beings are always imperfect? Inside human beings, there is godliness. Wake that godliness up. Move from one perfection to another and not from imperfection to imperfection.

You can see fault with everything, like milk gets spoilt and becomes curd and then butter. You can see first milk gets spoilt and becomes curd, and then curd gets spoilt and becomes butter. You can talk about only imperfections, or you can see progress from perfection to perfection.

Faith and alertness appear to be completely opposite in nature. When you are alert, usually there is no faith and you feel restless and insecure. When there is faith the mind is secure and rested and you are not alert.

There are three types of faith:

Tamasic faith, which is because of dullness. Like when you do not want to take responsibility or action and you say, 'Oh, it doesn't matter; anyway, God will take care of all these things!'

Rajasic faith, which is brought on by intense compulsion of desires and ambitions. Ambitions keep the faith alive.

Sattvic faith is innocent and is born out of the fullness of consciousness.

Faith and alertness, though apparently opposite in nature, are actually complementary to each other. In the absence of faith, there can be no growth, and without alertness there can be no correct understanding. Faith can make you complacent. Alertness makes you tense.

If there is no faith, there is fear. And when there is no alertness one cannot perceive or express properly. A combination of both is essential.

In gyan (state of wisdom), there is alertness without tension and faith without complacency. The purpose of education should be to remove the element of dullness from faith and the element of fear from alertness. This is a unique and rare combination. If you have faith and alertness at the same time, then you will become a true Gyani.

Our mind feels and perceives differently in the morning than it does in the evening. The placement of planets also affects the mind. Sometimes faith arises in the mind, sometimes hatred envelopes the mind. It is natural for different waves of emotions to rise in the mind. I am separate from all this, I am Atma. Contemplating on this is the sign of intelligence.

Let me give my own introduction. Shall I do that? I'm a child who refuses to grow up. That's a one-line introduction of myself. And I've seen that all of us, every human being has that child-likeness within us but it is buried under the debris of the past or concerns about the future. Our job or the job of anyone who is wishing good for the society is to remove this debris and allow this beautiful gift that Nature has embedded in us to blossom, the simplicity, the naturalness, the human values of compassion and friendliness. These don't have to be cultivated. These are there in us, and only need to be nurtured and brought to light again. And I would call this as spirituality.

See, we are all made up of both matter and spirit. Matter – amino acids, carbohydrates, protein, etc. Spirit is love, compassion, sense of belonging, all inclusive feelings, a broad vision about oneself, one's life, and the world. This is what is comprised of spirit and anything that uplifts spirit and the spiritual values, I would call that spirituality. What do you say? It is not some ritual or some belief system. It is much beyond that. It is the essence of good human being. In fact, there is not a single human being who does not want happiness, love or compassion in his/her life. In that sense, everyone is spiritual whether he/she recognizes it or not.

There is a saying in ancient India – The first sign of intelligence is not to speak at all. And suppose if you have lost the first sign then the second sign of intelligence is not to speak when a question is not asked. So, all our scriptures here in this land begin with a question. Whether you take the Bhagwad Gita, you take the Purana, or the Ramayana. Any scripture you see, any ancient text, Someone puts forward a question and then someone else answers. It could be a dialogue between a master and his disciple, husband and wife, between a group of seekers and a wise man. It has always begun in a question-answer form.

□

Making India a Spiritual Nation...

You know a question has got a single answer. But certain questions should not be answered. It should be made as a path. A road can be trodden many a time. Like this question, we will have to ask again and again in various circumstances. Why is not someone honest? Basically, it is lack of the sense of belonging. You know what; corruption begins outside the purview of the sense of belonging. No one can be corrupt with his/her own family, and if you extend it a little bit, to the near and dear ones. They're not corrupt with their friend circle, but when they put a boundary beyond that friend circle, when one thinks that only these people belong to me, then the people are no longer mine. Then the corruption begins. We have to educate people to expand a sense of belonging. The second aspect of corruption is insecurity. People who don't have friends try to find the security in money. Gosh, they don't know money is not going to bring him/her security. It's the company of right people who will bring more security in their life. You know if you go and ask a school boy or a girl how many friends he/she has, he/she will count on his/her fingers – 2,3,4,5. And I ask him/her, 'Hey, look you are spending 5 – 8 hours every day in a classroom of 50 – 100 kids, and you can't be friendly with everybody? And how are you going to live your life when you come out of the schools and colleges with the billion people, 6 billion people in the world?' So, the basic quality of being friendly is sort of foreign, sort of alien to our kids. Then what does happen? Insecurity creeps in. And to manage this insecurity, the only idea one gets is OK. I should have more money. So, then by somehow you amass money, be corrupt. So, first of all we have to spiritualize the politics, socialize the business and secularize the religions. If we can do these three things, society will be a better place to live in.

Every leader should see beyond his/her community and people. They should have a vision for the entire human race. You know, the Hindu priest, he should not only pray for the Hindus. He should pray for every human being. Similarly a Muslim or Christian priest, he should feel for the entire humanity then we have achieved the purpose of religion.

So, I would say secularize the religion, socialize the business. If every business undertakes corporate social responsibility of investing 1, 2, 3, 10 or whatever per cent of his/her profit in developing rural areas, I tell you this planet will have no hunger, will have no disease, will have no illiteracy. Because governments alone cannot do this, it is a social partnership with the NGOs and business organizations. They can do much more. So, socialize the business, bring social corporate responsibility and then spiritualize the politics. Now politicians, they had such integrity in the time of Mahatma Gandhi, they were respected highly. Today the situation is completely opposite.

You know, we need to spiritualize the politics. Politicians should care for people. I just want to share with you a particular story about my grandfather and grandmother. You know, when my grandfather met Mahatma Gandhi, he went and stayed with him in Sevagram for 20 years. My grandmother gave 10.5 kilo of gold. My grandmother was a beautiful lady. Those days the women used to don a lot of gold, covered from head to toe is all gold. Except the mangalsutra and a set of bangles, she willingly gave all her gold and she said, 'I will take care of the kids, you go and serve for the country.' So he went and stayed in Mahatma Gandhi's ashram.

You know, that sense of contributing and giving, taking pride in giving is missing today. If that comes up, there will be a big difference. Pride in giving, pride in non-violence are two things which are missing in today's education. If you see movies, one who is aggressive and loses his temper, is shown as hero. One who is calm, accepts everything and turns other cheek around, he is not considered a hero. This value shift has to happen. I'm just now coming from America where in Chicago we had a programme for school district children.

That was the most notorious school, 268 crimes happened in

the previous year. And when we introduced meditations, simple pranayama and simple values like making one new friend every day, and stand up and be compassionate, the crime incident rate this year dropped down to 60 from 268. They were amazed and the school district councillors came to thank me. 50 top officials of education said the techniques that we have introduced have brought real transformation. Otherwise, people there don't feel safe, you don't know what will happen there tomorrow, whether the child will come back with all the limbs intact. We need to bring this back. Sense of belonging, sense of caring and sharing, and pride in giving.

The understanding of the Gita should be, 'You work hard, you put your 100%, you look for the goals, you look to achieve the goals. But at the same time, you should have that faith, that confidence and relax.

You know, to achieve anything you need three types of confidence. First, confidence in yourself, Then you have no anxiety. It's very easy for me to handle this issue. I can do this. Second, confidence in the society around, people around. If you know that your team is good and they will achieve it, or if you have faith in the system that the system is continual and justice will be done to you. You know, if you have done well then you will definitely get well.

But if you don't have trust or faith in the system, if it's very corrupt then you will not pass it. So, we have to have faith and trust in the system. Third, trust in a power which is compassionate, higher power, the higher self, and this faith that it will always do best to people. These three types of trust can take us out of anxiety. For this, I would say take out a few minutes for yourself. Relax and Look back. How many times in the past you got stressed? You got some failures? You went through some failures and you achieved something. So, in the same way, now also you will achieve. That gives you that inner strength which is more needed at the time.

I would say it's like the cell phone. You know, for a cell phone you need to have the sim card. Correct? And you need the battery to be charged and you should be close to a tower. (Laughter) Should

be within the range. If any of this is missing then you can go on dialling, say hello and nothing, there'll be no response.

I would give you three suggestions to keep stress away. One, spend 10-15 minutes with yourself. What is it that you want? What is life all about? 50-60 years ago, where I was and where I will be 50 years later? What is my origin? What is my definition? Just don't look for an immediate answer. Even questioning yourself – 'What is life all about?' uplifts the spirit. This is what I would call as knowledge. Dwelling sometime with knowledge, you can read books like the Yoga Vashista, the Ashtavakra or even the Gita. Just a few lines or any other uplifting knowledge books. And then, 10-15 minutes of meditation. 10-15 minutes of meditation will give so much energy that it can refresh the brain, Refresh the spirit and energize the body. Fantastic! And the third thing is do some act of kindness, don't have to be in the routine. Take some time out. Do some random acts of kindness. Spend some time with music or art. These three things can bring you a lot of fulfillment and keep you away from stress.

Just imagine if in the world everyone walks like this – feeling insecure, depressed, unhappy, feeling lonely! What sort of company is that? What sort of world will we be in? What kind of institute will that be? Can you make any progress? First, you need to create the trust. That's the secret of management, and that begins with you having trust. When you walk around with your mind saying 'I don't trust you, I don't trust you, I don't trust you', the same thing reflects back to you. When we don't like being doubted by people, why do we keep doubt in everyone around us?

You know, banks give credit, I just take credit! You see a lamp is burning, it is not just the lamp but the wick and oil that burns, but the lamp takes the credit, correct? Any achievement, anything that's wonderful is a collective effort of so many. And you will see, in the collective effort, there is one inspiration, one wave, one energy, one divinity that supports and helps the progress. That component of life is called the Spiritual component. It is the lack of spiritual component that throws one either on one side of violence, or the other side of depression and suicidal tendencies.

Do you notice, when you are listening, you are also having a dialogue in your mind – Yes, No, how that could be? We are made up of seven faculties within us – The Body, Breath, Mind – The faculty by which you perceive. Intellect – that which agrees and disagrees, the judging aspect within you. The memory – Which often clings on to the negative. Given ten positive comments and one negative, your mind holds on to that one negative. Then Ego – That which makes you feel separate, and that which makes you feel motivated to do something. And then that reference point of all changes in life, something that doesn't change – The seven layers of life. A little bit about each layer of life brings the transformation. And that's all there is to the 'Art of Living'.

Leadership begins with an example. People ask me if I don't get tired for I travel so much. Haven't slept for four nights this last fortnight. Every night, I was travelling and visiting all the Tsunami-hit areas. I thought, 'Maybe I will get irritated if I haven't slept for the fourth night.' You know, to my surprise, I didn't. When people ask whether I don't get tired of doing so many things, I say I don't do anything which is not in my nature.

Living by example – the first quality of leadership, and being totally open and honest! If you did a mistake, say: 'okay, I did a mistake.' When you try to cover one mistake, it leads to a chain of mistakes. One mistake leads to another mistake. That weakens your whole system, weakens your working style, your environment. So, just being straight forward, open, honest and inclusive.

Often, we point out someone's mistake. You know why, because

their mistake hurts us. 'What you are doing, you shouldn't do it because it is hurting me.' This is what we often hear. When you go to correct someone's mistake with this attitude, it never gets corrected. So, what do you need to do? What you are doing will hurt you, so you better don't do it. Not because it is hurting me, but eventually it is going to hurt you, so you had better change. That brings transformation!

I would say, 'We need to put attention on three C's.' First, see your life in the context of time and space, the cosmology. How vast this creation is! How big this Universe is and how small our life is! Billions of years have passed and billions more to come. What is my position in context with this? You are living this life with 6 billion people on this planet right now! Do you feel you belong to him/her all? Do you feel at home with everyone? When you have that sense of belongingness, you start with that feeling, know that you have earned the customers everywhere. In fact, they become your family, an extended family. Sense of belongingness in any setup! Very important! Whether it is a corporation, NGO, social organization, religious organization, and a leader is to create that sense of belongingness, sense of responsibility.

After reciting 18 chapters of the Bhagvad Gita, Lord Krishna tells Arjuna, 'You think about it, analyze it, if it appeals to your mind and if you agree then you accept it.' This means the strength that is within us; the strength of the soul is what gives us this freedom. So now we have to utilize it in the right direction. So whenever we are happy and joyful, we should make an effort to spread this happiness, this joy to minimum ten other people. Will you all do it? Everybody?

An Ashram is a place where there is no shram/effort. Keeping the mind at peace and letting divinity flow through you is effortlessness. And when does that happen? When you are at ease with yourself and the surroundings. And this is, in fact, the significance of the Ashram – where you are at home.

When you have experienced inner peace, then either the Ashram has no significance or all the places become an Ashram for you. Yet till then, the Ashram and its vibrations, do have an impact. So, on this occasion of the 30th anniversary of the Ashram, be at home, be at Ashram, and be at peace with yourself. Wherever you are, make it an Ashram. Every home becomes an Ashram, this should be our wish!

Krishna says, 'Do your duty. I will take care of your sins. You just surrender. If you surrender then it's my responsibility to take care of your sins. Don't worry.' That's what I also say. Just come and participate in meditation, yoga and satsang, you will not have any worries in life. Just meditate and believe that you have left your sins here.

There is one proverb in India, 'Task gets accomplished with the Sattva, and not with the material.' So, in order to get something done, sattogun should rise. And what does one do to increase sattogun? With right food, right conduct, and relaxing your mind for some time – This is the first. Secondly, even if you face failure in spite of that, sattogun doesn't let your enthusiasm shatter, and when that driving force is still there, you don't even think of dropping out. Like if a gambler wins once, he develops that taste to win. And then he continues to play again and again with the wish to win, and even when some failure is encountered, he doesn't even think of dropping in between. Even during some failure, that strong conviction of achieving some good is there, and this conviction will be there when you have that dedication for the task. Like, with enthusiasm in action and peace in heart, people kept fighting for freedom for two centuries.

The ones who were fighting for freedom, they didn't get any money, they didn't steal anything, but did they leave the drive?

And a third factor, look for the reason of failure. Every failure is a step towards success. One reason can be some weakness in oneself or some weak point in the system, arrangements. Self-weakness – like someone is not able to present the work properly. For example, if you go for an interview, and say some words here and there, then

the interviewer develops a doubt if you would be able to do that or not. So, one doesn't get the job because of one's weakness. To get rid of one's weakness, enhance your abilities.

Each failure is a step towards success, so analyze what did you learn out of this? Did you flow with the emotions? You didn't consult those who are already into that profession? You didn't trust him/her, or you didn't keep faithful people with you. All these reasons could be there. So, to get rid of any weakness, enhance your ability, and go into the depth of knowledge of the field in which you wish to move ahead.

Amend the system or arrangements. Now, this is not in the hands of a single person. Like if corruption is to be checked, can you fight alone? Be with the group. Awaken that intelligence in people for that. Get people to move ahead with you. It has been rightly said, 'Sanghe Shakti Kaliyuge.'

In Kaliyuga, the power is in the team. People say that it is the peak of Kaliyuga, and it is as if truth has taken a backseat. If you feel like that, then work in a team. Take some people along and then see if the task gets accomplished or not. To enhance capability, you would have to do something yourself, go within yourself. Be in the world to get more people along, and be with yourself to gain abilities. Taking along both the fields, you will definitely get success in your tasks. If you have given all your trials, put in your 100 per cent and if, even then you didn't get success, then it is OK. Take some other work in your hands. But don't run away if you face failure for the first or second time.

First be more and more happy and then if some moments of unpleasantness creep in life – accept him/her. Don't get upset because you were upset sometimes in the past, and then you will always be happy.

It is quite natural to go towards violence for survival – it is a natural instinct. But, if self-confidence and vision are instilled in such a person, then you will find that the person walks with a vision in self-confidence without the fear of the problem of survival.

What is the crux of life? At least, first you start exploring within for that adventure! What should I tell you beforehand? The whole life is in search of some juice, some happiness. Where you feel happiness, solaced, be at peace there, relax there. And you get that joy when you look within. Meditation is such a joy! When the tiredness cracks away, you get that relaxation, that joy you are looking for.

Every confusion is a sign of growth, every time a pattern is broken. In such a case, just relax. In relaxation your intuition works. Rely on it.

Suppose you keep here many different vessels with different sizes. They have different capacities: one can have two litres, one can have ten litres, and one can have five litres. But the space is the same. The capacity of each vessel may be different. So what! But it is the same space which is inside, outside and which is everywhere. Our ability to do different things, our energy to do different things is immaterial to what we are. And this ability, this energy doesn't stay the same throughout life. See, when you were a baby your abilities were different, rather nothing. You could not help even yourself. Somebody had to care for you. And what happens when you get very old? Then also your abilities are different. So changing of our abilities, our thought is immaterial to the real you, to who you are. You are simply space, you are love, you are peace and this identification removes all other complexities in life. Otherwise, you will always find somebody is more capable than you and somebody is less capable than you. You are better somewhere and you are not in some others. When you compare yourself with others in the world, who are either living or dead or may be being born in the future, there will always be a difference. This is part of the world, part of the Universe.

You know you should have one policy, 'We will not do anything which is too difficult!' Be easy going, a happy go-lucky person. Why do you have to struggle? If being unhappy is easy, just go for it. If being miserable is the easiest thing and being happy is so difficult, why do you have to struggle to be happy! Got it? Go for the easiest, and the easiest is to be unhappy? NO! The simplest, the easiest thing is to be relaxed and happy. If you say why it is so difficult, we have to fix this a little bit. And that thing which fixes this is knowledge. Got it? And I tell you, it's easy!

What you say is exactly what is happening! You have said it! It will pass, it will pass definitely.

You know, if you are tired, you have not taken either enough water or too little sugar. Either too little energy or too much energy, or your system has some bugs or not any stress release. Any one of these can cause that. When you go deep in meditation, what happens? The stresses come out. When they come out, you feel either tired or feel like running away. All this is possible. If you take a few breaths or walk in the fresh snow, it will help. And take plenty of water, fluids, fruit, vegetables. All this would help.

If you are just beginning to meditate, restlessness comes up or you feel very sleepy. When stresses get released from your system, such a passage may be common. When stress release happens, the chemical or structural form in which stress was stored gets released, you get all these experiences. Your endocrine system readjusts itself, because we have violated our body in so many ways, so many times. We have not kept the balance; we have not honoured our own bodies, so jerks may happen. How many of you have found some jerks? Emotions may come up and you feel completely confused. All this may happen. It's not that it should happen. Sometimes it doesn't happen and you say, am I not releasing any stress? That person is getting stress released and I am so quiet. Don't compare your experience with that of anybody whatsoever. We all are so different. Everybody's nervous system is so different. And at different times, different experiences come to different people. So at any time, we should never compare our experiences with those of others and feel sorry or happy about it.

You know, people with schizophrenia, you think they are suffering, they are enjoying him/herselves! Ask me how many people I have encountered who have this problem. Sometimes they stop taking their medication because they stop having fun with that. See, there is no charm, no energy, no fun, so they stop medication. We have this experience. Many times parents or spouse came and left him/her in the Ashram. So we have dealt with him/her all. I tell you, they are really not suffering! They are in their own world. They are here in the world for you to serve him/her. And be patient, they increase your patience. They make you well grounded to your own reality. It's an experience to be with him/her. Because their mind are between two worlds – this world and another world, their realities fused and confused. They can invoke a lot of compassion from within you. And that is what you can do about it. Yes, they can do some physical yoga, dance, enjoy music and take a good walk. These are things you can engage him/her in.

□

Understanding Dreams...

Past impressions! You know, there are five types of dreams. Do you know about that? How many of you don't know?

One is your past impressions in the mind come to you as dreams. Second is your desires, ambitions, dreams come to you as dreams. Your unfulfilled desires come to you as dreams. Like you wanted to have hot chocolate and you sleep, you have hot chocolate in your dream. Have you had this type of dreams? Third type of dream is premonition. What is going to happen in the future, you get it in your dream. Everyone gets once in a while such dreams, premonitions. The fourth type of dream has nothing to do with you but the place you are in. Suppose you go and sleep in France, you get a dream in which everybody is speaking French, French words and faces that you have never seen before or sometimes the people who were there in that area or the impressions in that space come to you as dream. The fifth type is a mix of all these – a hotchpotch. That is what mostly dreams are. Ninety per cent dreams are of this category. You are riding a horse and suddenly the horse is inside a train. There is no logic to it and it all appears to be very perfect and really clear. Suddenly, the train transforms into a boat and the boat turns into a train! All these things can happen. This is all possible in dreams. So many possibilities because it's a mixture of all: your desires, past impressions, what may happen in the future and then the place. That's why you don't need to analyze too much. It's another form of stress release. Wake up!

Even that is written. Your asking this question is written too, got it? But me giving an answer for it is not written!

Come on! Animals are governed by instincts. They have no choice, they are programmed. But the human system is programmed with a possibility of either/or. Human system has the choice also programmed. But animals have no program of choice. Do you get what I am saying? In the program it is fixed that human beings can have the choice. Intellect is present in the human system which can make the choices. That means there is freedom also. Got it?

□

Understanding the Being Within

Remember one thing. The centre core of your existence is all positivity. All imperfection is only on the circumference. So deep inside you are pure, you are innocent, you are beautiful, and you must have total conviction in this. That is it. I am totally pure a hundred per cent, two hundred per cent positive. Deep inside you are simply a most adorable, most lovable person. You should have zero doubt about it. And whatever imperfections you may find in yourself or in others are only on the circumference. This conviction is most important in spiritual growth. Otherwise, someone blames you, you take the blame and then you burn with it. When you have this conviction, if anybody says anything to you, you will not care and will simply smile at him. You will not be an emotional wreck any time, because you are so solid and well founded in the self. And that is what the whole spiritual exercise is! Shudhohum, budhohum – You are pure, crystal-clear and solid. That conviction makes you rest so peacefully. If you are made by Nature, you are perfect. Everything in Nature is perfect. There is one school of thought which says find imperfection. Another school of thought is to move from perfection to greater perfection. That is what we understand. Praising each other and praising oneself, uplift the spirit all the time. Give criticism and stand up to criticism. If someone criticizes you, welcome that, knowing too well that whatever is the criticism is part of his perception or your projection. Imperfection is nothing but a projection or perception. From your side you have projected like that to the other person or that person has perceived you like that. Imperfection is nothing but your inability to project the way you are to others or the perception of other person towards you. That's it. Got it? All these practices you do are to get to this stage – Improving perception, observation and expression.

And that is it. It can never be a hundred per cent. It is relative, this is the thing. There can always be a chance for improvement in perception and expression. But there is no chance for any improvement in the being.

When mind is outward and is stuck in an outside event or incident, you have to retrieve it back. That's what you have to do. Either something good happens or bad, it stays in mind for some time, produces an impression in your consciousness. But nothing stays for long and it vanishes by time. The sign of waking up is that you don't hold on to it for long. Sadhana, meditation is the greatest tool for that.

Spirituality just means knowing that it is one consciousness. One-world family – this thought came from India. One side there is slum, the other side is scam. We have to remove slums. For that first we need to remove alcoholism. Nearly 60 per cent of a poor man's income goes in alcohol.

Yoga increases our qualifications – Yoga brings 'yogyata' (talents). Whatever we think that starts to happen. People have started recognizing this secret all over the world. Even in China, where they don't believe in God, they have asked us to start spreading the knowledge of yoga.

Human beings have responsibilities and needs. If needs are more and responsibilities are less, that is not a rich life. Meditation and yoga makes our body and mind active, our life rich. We have to have a quality life, a joyful life.

If our life is not joyous, there is no way we can take care of others. That's why we should use Yoga, Ayurveda and Siddha techniques.

I have a dream – everyone should have a proper house to live in.

The second is that caste conflicts should be erased. We should increase the love among human beings. We have forgotten these practices, and it is time to renew these.

If you have any worries, you have to leave them here; That's the rule of satsang, you cannot take your worries back. You can go only after you have dropped him/her here.

If you can win your mind, you can win the whole world! For this, meditation is necessary. The purpose of human life is to know who you are! This is spirituality.

There can be no appreciation for good forces if there are no bad forces. It is the presence of a villain which makes Hero a Hero. So, life is just a game.

If there is no evil, how can we recognize good?

Technology is a blessing. How we use it can make it a curse.

Let's talk of the common thread. The same Divine is in me and in the whole universe. There is no place which is not permeated by the Divine. In Sanskrit, 'Ishwaro gurur atmeti murti bheda vibhagine,' There is no difference between Guru, Divine and me. What is common in all three is what I am!

A child playing a game goes to his/her mother and plays or cries. That is surrender. The state of mind of the child is surrender. Another way to look at it is if there is something that we can't handle any more, we give up to the higher power. That is surrender.

Even with so much sorrow we are not able to let go in this world. How we would be able to let go if it was only full of joy. So, surrender in sorrow, do service in joy.

Some karma we have to experience, and some we can change. For example, when we cook some sweet, if there is too much sweet, we add some rava, if it is less we can add sweetening agent. But once you have put the rava on the fire, you can't turn it back. In the same way, some karma can be changed, some can't.

Take past as a lesson, and see what you can do in the future. That is why we should take past as destiny and future as free will, that is intelligence.

World peace comes with individual peace. If individuals become peaceful, communities become peaceful, then the leaders of the world will also become peaceful, and we can have world peace. When people have broad vision for the whole world, world peace is a possibility. We need to spiritualize the politics, socialize the business and secularize the religion.

You know, why are children all over the world so attractive? Because their presence is so pure! Their presence, their vibration is so positive and clean. As we grow older, we forget how to make our vibrations more positive. In our presence, in our vibration, there are stress, tension and worries. Ya? And that is where these breathing exercises, Sudarshan kriya, pranayama, meditation, help – All these help to uplift our spirit. Make us feel very positive.

We all are entitled to a violence-free society, disease free-body, confusion-free mind, prejudice-free intellect, trauma-free memory, and sorrow-free soul.

We need to wake up. When we are deeply relaxed, we suddenly realize that we are connected to this entire universe. We are part of this universe. You know, I feel at home wherever I go in the world. I am at home with everybody in the planet. I am sure everyone has this ability. Every child does it. And we have to invoke or awaken the childlike innocence in our hearts. To do this, we get doubts in our mind, first of all. The mind says, 'Is it possible?' Yes, it is possible. And then the doubt is, 'Whether I can do it? Maybe I cannot do it. Maybe it's not for me.' I would say, you should think of the impossible. You know if we dream of the impossible, one day we will make it possible. Ya?

You know, when I first came to Hamburg in 80s, we were doing meditation camp there with about 200 people. And I said, 'Let us all put an intention out there – East and West Germany should become one. We don't want these borders, fear and tension here. Let us put this intention.' At the end of that session, I said, 'You will see within a couple of years, it will become one. Within two years East and West will be one.' At that time Dr Aber Hart, Carl, Fetra, Riketta were all there. They said, 'It is not possible.' Everyone thought, 'Oh, Guruji is from India. He doesn't know what the situation is. This is an impossible thing to do.' But I said, 'It is going to happen before two years.' And that intention manifested itself. So, we need to put our intention. When our hearts are pure and in a calm state of mind, we put an intention and put attention on it, it will manifest. Nature has provided such a technology in our brain, in our consciousness. The ancient rishis in India, they called it sankalpa-siddhi. That means fructifying an intention, manifesting an intention. How is it possible? Only when the mind is absolutely still, calm and serene, intention gets fructified. And we all have this ability. But we have not learnt how to calm the mind. Though this knowledge was known to ancient people, they used to keep it as a secret. It was not given to everybody in the world. They used to wait for a capable and qualified student to come and learn. I felt that this should be given to everybody, because this will make everyone positive. I believe, 'Anything that is useful to people should not be the property of one community or one nation. It should belong to the whole world.'

You know, the 'World Health Organization' has declared that 30 per cent of Europe is suffering from depression. And they said, 'The second biggest killer in the next decade of the world will be depression'. In the next ten years, this will go up to 50 per cent with the stock markets crashing, value of money going down, uncertainty in every field… There is so much anxiety and uncertainty. People don't know how to handle the mind! That is why this knowledge is so essential. With this knowledge of meditation, breathing and mind, one can keep oneself happy all the time. Come what may! Isn't it so?

When do you need the strength? You need strength when everything is falling apart around you. That strength comes attending to your own breath, your own mind. It's so useful, I tell you! When people start learning about their own breath, they feel such a transformation, feel so blissful, feel that we all have a responsibility.

You know there are two types of joy. One type of joy is that you get while getting something. As a child, you always wanted to get something. Getting something used to make you happy. You know, we wanted to get toffees, toys, visit different places. But the mature joy is that you get when you give something. When you share, you feel happy. When you see a good movie, you force everybody, 'It's a very good movie. You must see it.' You tell everybody. The movie-maker is not giving you any commission. But you just feel good because you have seen a good movie and you want your loved ones to experience the same. This joy of sharing is much superior and the world is forgetting that joy of sharing, especially youngsters, isn't it? We have to bring it…just make him/her aware of it, that's all. Everyone has this tendency. They simply have to be encouraged.

That which you cannot express is Love.
That which you cannot reject/renounce is Beauty.
That which you cannot avoid is Truth.

When we are joyful, we do not look for perfection. If you are looking for perfection then you are not at the source of joy. Joy is the realization that there is no vacation from wisdom. The world appears imperfect on the surface but underneath, all is perfect. Perfection hides; imperfection flaunts itself.

The wise will not stay on the surface but will probe into the depths. The things you see are not blurred; it is your vision that is blurred. Infinite actions prevail in the wholeness of consciousness, and yet consciousness remains perfect, untouched. Realize this now and be at home.

One commits suicide out of sorrow, and tries to destroy the body. One tries to commit such a thing burdened with the sorrow, and in search of happiness. But committing suicide is like you removing your coat when you are feeling cold. There is only repentance after suicide, and one keeps on struggling to get a new body. Don't try to finish this body, and also don't hold on to it very strongly.

Inner joy and true happiness alone can stop the feverishness in society that arises through desires.

The most fortunate event that can take place in our lives is when we feel, 'I do not want anything, and I am here for you.' I have been bestowed with the good fortune of feeling this way right from the beginning. My wish is to see more and more people being able to think in this manner. Imagine how society would be if each member of the society thinks the same way! This feeling, this virtue is already there in everyone, but it is just hidden somewhere deep inside.

When the leader of a country feels in this manner, only then will the country progress; and when he is focused on the development of the country and its people, it is impossible that the needs of the leader are not fulfilled. But if we focus only on our needs, then we don't give ourselves and our abilities a chance to blossom. We must always believe that our needs will be fulfilled.

This does not mean that when you have some needs, you suppress him/her saying, 'I do not want anything.' This is a feeling that arises from a state of contentment or fulfilment, and not by neglecting or suppressing your needs, and fulfilment comes from spiritual knowledge. When you pay attention and focus on the highest knowledge, then your needs are fulfilled even before time.

Inner joy and true happiness alone can stop the feverishness in society that arises through desires. This kind of inner joy and happiness can only be achieved through knowledge. It is a matter of joy that The Art of Living is bringing together the various communities of the world. The core of every religion and culture is love, and The Art of Living is also based on the same principle of LOVE, 'I do not want anything and I am here for you.' More and more people around the world should be able to develop the ability to say this.

If everyone starts to think like this, this world will become heaven. If everyone only thinks of taking something from someone, then we will continue to see the current world situation.

We are developing the world to make it heaven, and it feels very good to see it happening. So every day we move forward with this belief that 'I am yours.' Love, action, fun and celebration are all present in this knowledge. All of this comes from the knowledge.

For success or work to get done, there are five things you require. First, the intention of the person who is doing, then availability of the instruments or things needed to do the work, third is the willingness or mindset to do the work. Then doing the work at the right time, there is a time to do the work, if you don't do it at the right time then there is no use. If you sow seeds in February then there is no use, you then cannot say that I sowed the seeds but nothing has come. You have to wait till April after the rains and then you sow the seeds and yield the results. So time is a very important factor. When we came to this Ashram, this whole land was barren; there was not one leaf or one tree on this land. Today see, how many trees and plants are there and these trees did not come in one day, so many people have put lots of effort and after some time the trees grew. So this is

how time is an important factor and then grace. Without the grace of the Divine there will be no success, that is why you do seva, sadhana, satsang and in time you will get the fruits of all your efforts. Okay! None of your efforts will go waste that you should be assured about, if not now you will see the results later.

Wealth is not just having money. You can have a big balance, you can have a big estate but on your face if you are stressed and you're so miserable, no one can call you prosperous. Prosperity is not just having a fat bank balance. Prosperity is in acknowledging the magnanimity of life, honouring life. The confidence in a person shows his richness. What is wealth supposed to do to you? Enhance confidence right but if wealth has created weakness then it is no wealth, if wealth has created sickness then it's no wealth, if wealth has created conflicts then it is no wealth, right! So one type of wealth is wisdom, knowledge is wealth, health is wealth, confidence is wealth, valour is wealth. If you have confidence you can manage anything, you can handle any situation that is wealth.

This is a state of consciousness where you realize things are not happening because of your effort, it is happening due to some law, due to some power in the creation which is making everything happen. When you have given your 100 per cent, physically, intellectually… then you realize you are not doing, but things are happening.

It's like asking – should I feel thirsty? If you feel thirsty, you will ask for water. Should I ask for water has no meaning, since you have already indicated that you're thirsty. If a prayer comes, let it come. It just comes up.

I am feeling grateful to be in the city of Saints. The ten Gurus of Sikh tradition have made so many important contributions and sacrificed their lives for mankind. The grace of the Masters, from

Sri Guru Nanak Dev to Sri Guru Gobind Singh is showering on this holy city. Doing kirtan (satsang) we adore the old tradition. It is important today to solidify the voice of love. The one with a clean heart and enthusiasm can do this. The land of the Punjab is the face of the whole of India. Yet, the holy land is suffering because of evils like drug addiction and female foeticide. Seeing this, there arose a sankalpa in the mind to have a drug-free Punjab – Let the kids, elderly and everybody be free from addictions, and let the mind find peace and true intoxication in the Divine.

One more important issue that needs to be brought into light is to preserve the Indian seeds. How many of you suffer from body aches? (An astounding number of people raised their hands). This is because of consuming food with pesticides. So, preserving local seeds and adopting organic farming is the remedy.

Youngsters need to be awakened to the actual essence of the religion. We somewhere fail to present the actual relaxing and soothing aspect of spirituality or religion.

If the very root is spoilt, the tree withers. We need to respect our tradition, our roots. Sikh means one who learns and we can all learn something from everybody. We need to learn hospitality from the Japanese, precision from Germans, etiquette from the English and marketing from America and from India, human values.

Love is beyond language. When the heart finds a way, language is no longer a barrier. Yet to realize love we need to remove the label of being unhappy from our hearts. 'I am unhappy' – We put and encourage this label on us. And why do we do that? Because of stress and conflicts that arise due to it. We have to work to make each home free from stress. But before that, we have to free ourselves of the conflicts that are happening inside our minds. This is self-knowledge. When stress is there, we become angry, making ourselves and others sad. To get rid of stress from the very roots, we need to

meditate regularly for some time. When you sit to listen to kirtan, just be immersed in that. But if your mind keeps running and disturbing you even when you sit to cherish kirtan, then pranayama, yoga and meditation all come to aid.

Violence-free society, disease-free body, quiver-free breath, confusion-free mind, inhibition-free intellect, trauma-free memory, sorrow-free soul, and an ego that encompasses all are the birthrights of everybody on the planet. We have been bestowed with knowledge since ages, but the tragedy is that we don't know our own tradition. In Tamil Nadu, nobody knows about the sacrifice of the ten Gurus. The kids have studied a little about Sri Guru Nanak Dev and Sri Guru Gobind Singh in their school curriculum. Similarly, nobody here knows that there were 63 great saints in Tamil Nadu. There have been so many sages in so many countries. Five years ago, we held an exhibition about ten Gurus and that brought awareness. What is our heritage? What are our roots? Self-knowledge is the very base of our ancient tradition. The very basis of science is spirituality, the ancient knowledge of our scriptures.

Corruption has reached all fields. This is a burning issue that requires to be given attention. What society do we want to leave for the coming generation? If we do not give him/her a society better than ours, we will miss to fulfil our responsibility.

Satsriakaal, honouring the truth that is beyond time and honouring the treasure that is within each one of us, is one of the best greetings in the world. When you identify the treasure within, worldly prosperity automatically follows. The inner richness is anyway there, but that treasure is to be identified. There is a science behind the sound of Omkar. Scientists have found that the frequency of the earth rotating around its axis is the same as that of OM. The graph plotted for the two frequencies is the same. So, whenever we chant OM, our vibes match with that of the earth's natural frequency, the natural law.

The same is said by our ancient rishis as well. Maharishi Patanjali has said, 'If you want to get rid of sorrow, contemplate on that one Divine principle/ God.' Think of that ultimate bliss called the Divine. Japji Sahib starts with that – Ek Omkar, The one Omkar. All sorrow diminishes, doubts shatter and you gain health cherishing that one principle. That is why in Buddhism, Jainism, and Sikhism and in Hinduism, 'OM' has got a special place. The same is true for Taoism and Shintoism. Even in Islam and Christianity, we see a glimpse of 'OM' in Ameen and Amen respectively.

When you are content and not bombarded with your own needs, you gain the ability to bless, and we need to learn that skill of being content. This can only happen through meditation. We have this beautiful tradition where we go to seek the blessings of our elderly in all functions or occasions. This is very scientific. Ideally, elder ones are expected to be content, and hence they should have the ability to bless. Yet today that is missing somewhere. And contentment does not mean being lethargic or not working, and also one is not to wait till getting old to feel contented. There should spring a wave of contentment in the mind. Keep on doing your work but have a sense of satisfaction in the mind. Some time in life, one should reach this stage of feeling, 'I am contented.' Without contentment, that power does not wake up within you. Many people who have done the blessing course have this experience that whatever good they wish for others, it gets accomplished. How many of you have this experience? (Again many hands in the air.) Spend your life celebrating and enjoying doing sadhana, seva and satsang. Be happy and make others happy!

Let the light in my life, the enthusiasm and wisdom around me always be there. I take the light of life into me. I accept wisdom and love.

What is pooja? Reciprocating what Divinity is doing to us. God

makes the Sun and the Moon go around us, showers flowers, rain and fruits. The imitation of that Divine expression is called pooja. Pooja is the most natural way of showing one's gratitude.

Divinity is everywhere like the air. Yet, you feel the air near the fan. Similarly, Divinity is everywhere but you feel it more near the fan. Knowledge, yagya and Guru are like the fan. Near these you feel the presence of Divinity.

You take shower in the morning to clean your body. After that you do all the daily activities. You don't have to keep on taking a shower throughout the day. It is like that. You meditate and calm your mind, then go on with other activities. It is not easy to keep yourself undisturbed but it will happen if you keep doing the practices regularly. Then keeping yourself calm will become easy.

You know, nobody compels you to give, but your giving brings a certain amount of satisfaction.

I say two things that you have to have in life. One is smile more, serve as much as you can and not to worry.

Ego is feeling uncomfortable in the presence of someone else. Self-confidence is, feeling at home. Being natural is antidote to ego, and being natural is so complementary to confidence. It goes with confidence and is inseparable from confidence. When you are confident, you are natural. If you are natural, you are confident.

There is no doubt that you need some money for your day-to-day survival. But money cannot buy you happiness. It's knowledge or wisdom that brings you happiness.

You know, this is our brand mark. Our logo is smile. If you see somebody and he/she is not smiling, and he/she says he/she has done 'Art of Living', don't believe him/her. I am sure, all those who are here, who have truly done it will agree with me.

You know, we should have a goal in life. My goal is to bring happiness to more and more people. If we sit and keep thinking of ourselves all the time, we'll be depressed. We should see, 'How can I be of service? How can I be of use to others?' This thought is very useful. Very, very, very useful. Ya?

'Art of Living' provides a platform for everyone to come together and do some service. You know, when United Nations announced, 'Stand up and take action' – they wanted tree planting; 'Art of Living' volunteers have planted 55 million trees around the globe.

We all can jointly do some service activity. Reduce violence, reduce stress, create a sense of belongingness, and spread the positive vibration of love and peace. Shall we all do this together? Is everyone committed to do this?

Advaita is quantum physics. Quantum physics says that this is all atoms or this is all wave function, vibration (referring to the space and things around). That's exactly what Advaita says. So, the whole universe is made up of one substance. Me, you, she, he…everybody and everything is made up of one substance. And the nature of that substance is bliss. This is what Advaita is.

Just a glimpse of that experience gives you so much strength and stability, that nothing can shake you; nobody can take the smile from you.

Advaita – Knowing that there is something in you that is not changing. A little experience of silence, calmness and meditation will give you enormous courage from within.

You know, when we started in India, it was a small programme. We had no resources and manpower. But we had a vision – We have to reach many people in the world. So, in these 30 years we have reached millions of people. So, it is possible.

You know, the cell phone has reached the whole world. If the cell phone could reach the whole world, do you think wisdom and compassion cannot reach the whole world? We must make an effort. OK?

Don't make an effort to regain it. Listen to your heart. Trust can never be lost. Doubt as much as possible, but truth always stands up to the doubt. Truth is so strong that doubt cannot destroy it. So, it is good to doubt. And the trust which moves through the doubt and stands, that is true trust.

You sowed a coconut tree two years back and it has grown today. The same way, until the impression of your previous done karma is there on your mind, that karma manages to exist. That impression can only be erased through meditation, pranayama and service. All this is there on the mind only. Karma is nothing but an impression on the mind. When you wake up and see that mind is a part of you and it is your mind, but you are not your mind, and you have an untouched existence which is much greater than your mind, then all karma automatically dissolves.

We are to fight against the evil of ignorance. There are so many problems in the society today – corruption, exploitation of environment, starvation, powers opposing spirituality, and anti-humanity powers. These all have to be defeated.

Beyond space? Me!

The Guru Granth Sahib is a very sacred scripture. One should definitely respect it. Guru is not a person; Guru is knowledge, whether it is in a scripture, a person, or consciousness. That Guru tattva is to be revered and believed in. Our mind only creates complication, otherwise there is no dilemma. The Guru Granth Sahib contains the crux of all scriptures. So, respect the scripture. There is no question of choosing here.

Mother is our first Guru.

School teacher is our second Guru.

Then music teacher is also a Guru.

And one who gives the knowledge of the truth is Satguru.

When Guru tattva wakes up in life, it is not partially awakened; it stays completely. So, live naturally. Rejoice and live in love and joy.

This race of more and more is killing us. More and more and more – How can I get more? Relax my dear. We don't even have enough time to enjoy what we have. We should think how I can be more useful to the society, how I can serve more. One who is always thinking of getting something is like a beggar. Everything comes to the one who thinks how she/he can contribute more to the society. There won't be any lack for such a person.

It is easy to be popular but it is difficult to be a Guru. A Guru has a responsibility.

We are made up of both matter and spirit. The spirit needs spirituality, the body (matter) has some material needs and our spirit is nourished by spirituality. You cannot live life without spirituality. Do you want peace? Do you want joy? Do you want happiness? We think spirituality means going to a temple, church or a mosque. Spirituality is human values. Without human values, life is meaningless. If someone asks, 'Why do you need human values?' You would say,

'It is a silly question. There is no point in living like an animal, when you are a human being. Living with human values is being human.'

Man has some needs and takes responsibilities. When needs are less and responsibilities are more, life is good. When needs are more and responsibilities are few, life is not so good. Some needs could be there but if you take very few responsibilities, then you are unhappy. It is not a spiritual life. Bharathiyaar, Kamraj and Gandhi took responsibility for the whole country and see the way they lived – their needs were minimum.

Take more responsibility. If the father does not take responsibility for the children and their needs, will they listen to him? Only those who take responsibility, gain authority. People in politics ought to take responsibility for the whole nation. But if they rise in power by corrupt means, the fall is certain.

When we take more responsibility, how do we manage him/her? The ability to take responsibility beyond our capacity and managing it comes from spirituality.

If you sow a neem tree, will mangoes grow in it? You have tc be intelligent. You may be a good person, yet are you intelligent? I you're good and you put your hand in fire, you will still get burnt You have to be good and intelligent. Use your buddhi (intelligence and use it well. We use our intelligence only for corruption and nc to be a good person. We think we are good; others are bad. It's nc like that. There is some goodness in everybody. Spirituality increase it. Even when problems are there, they teach us something – we g depth. Happiness brings expansion; difficulties bring depth.

Take both the modern and the ancient, and move ahead. Tl roots are spirituality, our tradition and culture. The leaves and branch are science. When you take science and spirituality together, th you will progress in life.

Sometimes in the name of spirituality, we follow superstitions or thinking we are scientific, we ignore our traditions. That is not the way. You must take the middle path. Honour and respect our traditions, have a scientific outlook and whatever good we can do to others, keep doing.

If you think something is your duty, there is no love in it. Sometimes you even get headaches because you feel burdened by the duty. When you do something with love, that is the best. When you take responsibility with love, then it is not a burden to you. It becomes like a pooja and that is the best. If you think that doing pooja itself is a duty, then there is no benefit in doing it at all.

If a father thinks, 'I have to get my daughter married somehow and get rid of my responsibilities' then it becomes a burden. But if he thinks of her marriage with love, then the whole event is a celebration and there is joy for everybody. So, take responsibility with love and take responsibility for the whole world. Start with small steps. First your family, then neighbours, society, village – nobody should be sad in your village! This attitude will make your heart blossom. When the heart blossoms, there is happiness. Divinity resides in a blossomed heart. You don't have to go anywhere and search for the Divine. His home will be in your heart.

We are exploiting the planet, using atom bombs, bursting him/her under water – so many nuclear weapons are being tested secretly under the water like this. The earth cannot bear it. Trees are being cut, so many toxins are being pumped into the ground, the earth is being mined and all the minerals are being removed – all this has to change. We must promote chemical-free farming methods. Our country's corn is small. Imported corn is bigger. Our rice grains are small, imported grains are larger. But our grains are much more healthy. We must protect our indigenous seeds. Our cow's dung and urine have medicinal properties. Protect desi cows and seeds. Imported

hybrid seeds give good yield for the first two or three years but deplete the soil completely. Thousands of farmers in Maharashtra committed suicide because of this. We must encourage the natural methods of farming.

Think carefully! If everything you wish for comes true, you will be asking 'why!' very soon! A king prayed to God to grant him a boon – that everything he touched should turn to gold. God granted his wish and he was very happy – but only for a few minutes. He was thirsty and wanted water. It turned to gold as he touched it. His food turned into gold and even his little daughter, when he touched her. The king became very disturbed and prayed that the boon be taken away.

Just look back and see – as a child, what did you want to become? An engine driver? Nowadays children have many toys. Around 30-40 years ago, the only thing a child wanted to be was an engine-driver or a pilot. Many things that you desired, you have stopped liking it now. The Divine will give what is best for you. Move ahead with that faith. If you have a desire, don't think that you should not pray for it. Just think – Let me get this, or something better.

Whichever direction you take, you will meet at some point as the earth is spherical. Communism and spirituality may seem to be opposing to each other but they will meet eventually.

Did you know that the Chinese government has added the need for spirituality in the Chinese Constitution? Prosperity, development and spirituality must be made available to every person in China.

You know, very few people hate spirituality. Look into the depth of your heart. There is either faith or fear in the Divine. What is the most important principle of communism? That everybody should get everything. Spirituality also says the same thing. See others as yourself. See the same God in all.

We make the difference. Some get 'A' grades or 'B' grades in school. We may have different talents and qualities. Some can lift 100 kilograms, some 10 and some cannot even lift 2.

Each person is unique in what he/she can do but at another level, everyone is the same. The blood in every person is red. Whatever breed a cow may be, the milk will be the same colour.

No two people will have the same fingerprints. If you look at our qualities and talents, we are all unique. At the level of love, we are all the same. There is no difference.

A small child will not eat ten idlis. If you give an adult, a small cup and spoon, will it do? Capacities are different, yet everyone is the same.

While watching television, what is more important? Seeing or hearing? You need both.

In the same way, in life too, we need both.

Spirituality transcends gender. Men and women are equal. There are many vacancies here for women who would like to become swamis as well! They should come to the forefront as well.

If you have ego, keep it in your pocket. Don't try to destroy it because that effort will only increase it. Be natural like a child. If it's there, it doesn't matter. When you feel separation or distance between yourself and others, then ego arises. We don't have ego with our family or those who are closest with us. Similarly, we don't have ego issues with people whom we don't know at all. It happens only with people we know a little. We develop ego. If everybody belongs to you, or nobody belongs to you, then there is no ego.

It is important to have child-like naturalness. When we are worried about what other people are saying about us, then there is ego. Even when you are doing good, there will be some people who will find fault with it. Similarly, there will be people to praise even

if the person is corrupt. So, don't worry about it. If you make a mistake, accept it. That is intelligence. In the same way, others can also make mistakes. Don't wait for him/her to ask for forgiveness. You forgive and move on. A mistake happened. Drop it. Don't keep thinking of past mistakes and chewing on it like gum. It is like churning up a pile of garbage. You must save your mind at all costs.

If you save your mind, then you can be free from desires and needs. When you can bless others, even their needs are fulfilled. That's why people take blessings from the elders of the house. As you grow older, you become more content. But that is not the case all the time. As people grow older, they collect worries and desires. Only when you are free from worries and desires, you gain the capacity to bless. At some point, you have to say, 'I am content'. That strength comes from spirituality.

When you realize who you are, all your needs are fulfilled. Your biggest enemy is your mind. That is why we do so many things to calm the mind. Take blessings and be happy.

Many millions have benefitted from the Sudarshan Kriya. Many, many are waiting. Take a sankalpa – 'Let the whole world also get the joy that I have got.'

This is a tricky question but I am not going to get caught! If your wife says something, you will say, 'Let me listen to my Guru' and if your Guru says something, you will say, 'What to do, my wife does not agree!' Finally you will do only what you want! This has been the case with man always! So I say, 'Choice is yours, blessings mine!'

When you're in activity, there will be fatigue in the body, the energy levels can go down. Sometimes this happens due to the effect of time as well. However, we must simply continue and not stop. A little pranayama and meditation can restore your energy levels and refresh you. This is where satsang is so important. We are recharged when we sit in satsang and can do seva with renewed energy.

Realization is just that I am not the body but I am much more than the body. I have been here before this birth and I will continue to be there after my death as well. If someone realizes this, that's it. But that only they can say, others cannot judge for him/her.

You know what the word Radha means? Radha means 'back to the source'. Dhara means flow; flow from the source is called dhara and when you read dhara the other way around, it is Radha. When water flows down, it is called dhara, and when water goes back from where it started flowing, it is Radha.

A 2-year-old child would not be so insecure, it may be your own projection. Sometimes you project yourself too much on what the child is feeling or saying. Especially grandparents have a lot of projection on the children. Grandpa will say my 6-month-old baby looked at me and said, 'Grandpa you don't go walking today, you stay with me,' and all that he was saying with his own eyes. The baby doesn't even speak but grandpa feels that he says everything. A lot of it will be your own projection.

If you feel your child is a little jealous, sibling jealousy will be there. If you feel that, then you pat him/her and give him/her a little more attention.

Tadap hi ishwar hai! (Longing is the Divine)

First of all, don't label everyone as cunning and corrupt. Then you will only see him/her in that light. Do not label people like that even if they are like that. Your sankalpa or your thought can bring

up the worst in him/her. However, if your sankalpa is good even in the people who appear to be worst, goodwill come out of him/her.

Today one of our teachers from Srinagar called me; he completed a YLTP course of 50 youths. He was mentioning that the transformation was so much in the youth. The district collector came for the closing ceremony and said, 'This is a miracle. What has happened to these youths here? So much transformation.' The youth were saying that you have never given us this kind of spiritual education before and you blame us that we do this and we do that, but nobody ever taught us inner peace.

So it is up to us to bring out the best in others, often we criticize others saying, 'You are hopeless', but you know there are some good things as well; you have to give him/her some hope. Bring out the Divine qualities in the people around you; take this as your mission. I am not telling you to be naïve. Be careful; at the same time bring out good qualities.

Play is nature. When you are happy what you do is play. When you play you have no need. That is why you play. If you are full of needs you only work, you can't play, do you get it? Games can come when you have free time. Play becomes part of your life when your needs are fulfilled. Consciousness is full and its nature is playfulness. The Divine's nature is being playful.

Caring for the environment is a big part of The Art of Living. Plant trees; use less plastic, if possible, no plastic and use cloth bags. These are all very valid things to know. Keep the environment clean, if you find people littering the streets you should try to educate him/her. If you have free time wherever you find any littering, you stand there and call a few people and tell him/her, 'Let's clear this place.' Do something like that.

How to free yourself from the grip of storms? This is the only basic problem in this universe. The first thing is to become aware of it and stop regretting it. Like waves come and go, storms in your life too will subside. No one storm can be there for ever. One storm comes and subsides, another comes and subsides and it goes on. As the storm subsides, you experience that inner

cool, soft, delicate aspect of yourself. In that space of calm, all the anxiety, fear, feverishness lose their grip on you and you become yourself again. Love dawns.

Humour is the buffer that saves you from humiliation. If you have a good sense of humour you can never be humiliated. And if you refuse to be humiliated you become invincible. Humour brings everyone together, while humiliation tears him/her apart. In a society torn with humiliation and insult, Humour is like a breath of fresh air. A good sense of humour relieves you from fear and anxiety. Humour should be coupled with care and concern.

Mere humour without care and concern or appropriate action often irritates those who come to you with serious problems. Humour can keep the spirit high, yet if overdone it leaves a bad taste. Humour without wisdom is shallow. Humour with wisdom creates an atmosphere of celebration. Humour without sensitivity is satire – it comes back to you with more problems.

The wise use Humour to bring wisdom and to lighten every situation. The intelligent use Humour as a shield against humiliation. The cruel use Humour as a sword to insult others. The irresponsible use Humour to escape from responsibility. And fools take Humour too seriously! To make an effort to be Humourous is nonsensical.

Humour is not just words, it is the lightness of your being. You do not have to read and repeat jokes — just being cordial and light-hearted brings out authentic Humour. Taking life itself not too seriously (because you will never come out of it alive!).

Having a sense of belongingness with everybody, including those who are not friendly.

Practising yoga and meditation, having unshakable faith in the Divine, and in the laws of Karma.

Being in the company of those who live in knowledge and are Humourous.

Have the willingness to be a clown!

Embrace Humour! Humiliation will not touch you!

□

Understanding Mistakes

Blessed are those who don't see a mistake as a mistake....!!! But it is hard not to see your own mistake. Outwardly, you may justify yourself or prove your innocence to someone else, but a mistake pricks conscience. Do not justify yourself. Instead, feel the prick of the mistake. That very pinch will take you out of the mistake.

A mistake means something that brings misery to you in the long run. So, why would someone knowingly commit a mistake?

While pointing out a mistake to someone, do you consider him as separate from you and go on pointing out his error or do you make him feel a part of you? When you point out a mistake to someone, does it make him more stressed, or does it create more awareness in that person? Often you do not point out someone's mistake when it is required. Not pointing out a mistake – with due consideration to time and place – is also a mistake.

When you make a new mistake, it is not a mistake; you have learnt a valuable lesson. But when you keep doing the same mistake over and over, it is a BIG mistake. A mistake simply means you have missed taking a lesson that has come your way.

Do not lament over your mistake. Just take the lesson from it. You will not be judged by your mistakes, but by your virtues. Mistakes are of the earth. Virtues are of the Divine.

A wise person is the one who learns from others' mistakes.

Less wise is the one who learns from his own mistakes.

The fool keeps making the same mistakes again and again and never learns from him/her.

When mind is free from lust, greed, possessiveness, arrogance,

etc., when the mind is in the pure form with which we were all born, then nature listens to you. You are a child of Nature and Nature loves you. When that manifests, when you are clear then two things happen – your wishes get fulfilled and you can fulfill others' wishes as well.

Rapid Fire with the Master

Night Life: All nights are in satsang. Appointment with the Divine.

Solitude: To be practised amongst the crowd.

The forgotten language: Impermanence of life.

The pathless path: Meditation.

Abhyasa (Practice): Is doing what you have known to be correct.

Desirelessness: is an outcome of joy.

Holiness: Your very nature.

Apologizing: Brings comfort to the ignorant.

Insult: Experienced by one who has never gone in.

Stealing: Worth doing with great things.

Sensitivity: Makes you human.

The Unconsciousness: The mother of all problems.

Sermons: Fruits that nobody picks or claims.

Swami: One who has established in oneself.

Nightmare: Experienced by one who has never done 'Art of Living'.

Political will: Serious deficit in resolving conflicts.

Ideology: Many keep it in their safe lockers, and never use it.

Cunningness: Has become so cheap in society where there is no spirituality.

Witness: It brings stability in emotions.

Assassination: Done by foolish people to bring suffering on him/herselves.

Justice: All that is – Just is.

Some think God is money. Many think money is God and very few know that God Himself is money. God is love and when you have richness of love in you, you will see how abundance flows in life. There is a saying in Sanskrit: 'Udyoginam purush sindh mupayi tilaxmi' God comes to you in the form of money – wealth is a consort of God. The consort of God, spirit of God comes to you as abundance when you put effort, to one who is working and not to one who is lazy. And one who has confidence and courage. So the one who has courage and confidence, and who puts in effort will get money. Don't keep buying lottery tickets and sit at home. This is the biggest problem – you want money but you don't want to do anything. So we have to put in effort. Money is just a means not an end in itself. You will need that but is it everything? No. You may have a lot of money but if you can't eat, you can't sleep well at night then that money is of no use. It loses its utility. So many people come here who have a lot of wealth and are depressed. They want to quit everything, their job, everything.

The World Health Organization (WHO) says that in the next 20 years, 40-45 per cent of the population will be depressed. What's the point in having so much money and prosperity in the world when so many people are getting depressed? That's why you need to have balance in life, balance of material and spiritual life, isn't it? Often people think spirituality means do nothing and sit quietly. No, it is not so. You should work. Even in the ashram there are 600 people who work day and night. There is no Sunday and no Monday for him/her and they work round the clock. People come here all the time and they work. Kitchen people are working so hard. The kitchen never takes rest. You have any idea how much food they cook every day when there is no big programme. 600-700 kg of rice is being cooked daily, 70 kg of salt is put in, and 100 kg of vegetables are cut every day. So much of work they do. The housing department works tirelessly. And they are still smiling. And there are people who go and work in the fields. They are working in slums. There are teachers who are working worldwide. They work day and night. In Karnataka itself, we have 78 slums and there are many different classes being run, educational classes, computer classes. Seva is a part of spirituality

and definitely you can't do charity with an empty bowl. You need money for service. But here nobody worries about money and charity happens, everything happens spontaneously. So these are some of the things we need to keep in our mind. You have money, you earn money, it's good but you should keep aside some part for charity, whatever your capacity is 3-10 per cent, keep it aside. Along with it do your spiritual practices daily.

Once in a year, keep seven days completely for spirituality and then you don't sit and calculate money. You come here and be 100 per cent here, and take care of your health, do yoga, pranayama, meditation and learning. It is a very common experience when businessmen come here leaving their jobs for some time and do seva, meditation and the advanced course, they start getting better contracts. Their wealth on the other side starts increasing. What they used to get putting in a lot of effort, starts to happen with very less effort. That is when sattva in you rises. Sattva is positive harmony within you and when that dwells up, your work outside also becomes smoother and better.

When you say a word, you have already heard a definition for it. I would say enlightenment is a connection with the universal spirit, realizing that you are part of it, you are that. Living unconditional love without any effort, you don't have to put any effort for that. Being like an open book, being natural and all these qualities are there in every individual. It only needs a little nurturing and then it starts blossoming. So when you walk, walk like you are enlightened, you are open, you are like a child, and you are free – emotionally, mentally and intellectually. Enjoy the freedom. When you don't have any cravings and aversions of your own, then you can give yourself a certificate that you are enlightened. But you should be over all your cravings and aversions. Clear heart, clear mind and clarity in action are all part of enlightenment. If you look at a child of two-three years, or a baby of six months – there is unconditional love in his eyes. Every baby has all these qualities but minus wisdom. When you grow old, keep all these qualities in you like innocence, and have the depth of wisdom along with it. That is what it is.

The intellect may not understand but the subtle body understands the depth of Mantras. And the vibrations that are produced are doing good to all the subtle layers of existence. This energy creates benevolence, benefits the whole mankind, washes away our bad karma, promotes harmony in the world and desires get fulfilled. Desires get fulfilled when there is strength in the subtle. These bring us close to self-realization and also to achieve success in the world.

Unhappiness is due to two things, one is the lack of resources in some parts of the world; if they get water they will be happy, if they get food they will be happy. In the other part of the world it is the lack of spirituality. In one place, the body is starving, so there is unhappiness, and in another place, the soul is starving and so there is unhappiness. We at The 'Art of Living' have to do both jobs, provide food to the body and food to the soul and that's what we are doing.

It is intuition, don't think there is an eye opening like this and something is popping up from your head. You get a bump or a hole in your forehead, no! You know you close your eyes, still you feel some light; you may see or you may feel, it can be both ways. If someone says, 'I am going to open your third eye and this and that, just don't go into those things.' I tell you, definitely not, it is simply hoax because I have seen so many people claiming to open the third eye and nothing happens really, people get a headache, incurable headaches many times and you get into problems. You know many such cases come to us for repair, so if someone says, 'I want to open your third eye,' tell him/her, 'Thank you very much; I am happy with two eyes.' The deeper you go in meditation, your intuitive ability develops.

You know the third eye is associated with alertness and awareness.

When you are alert, awake, more into knowledge then naturally the energy has moved from the lowest chakra to the highest. The lower things no more interest you. You know when you are very alert and awake the sexual energy has transformed itself into a different quality of consciousness. The sexual energy is when the back portion of our brain, our head is activated. Alertness, perception and awareness happen when the front portion of the brain is activated; the pituitary and pineal glands are getting activated. In the brain also, they are on the opposite sides of each other. So, it is myth logically said when the third eye opens then the gross desires simply evaporate, not that it is bad but they simply don't make much sense any more. That is why the intellectuals and the highly spiritual oriented practitioners always put something on the forehead, some sandalwood paste because they are focusing; doing some yoga and meditation, so they put some sandalwood paste to cool the forehead, to cool it a little bit.

When the frontal lobe of the brain becomes more active, more alert, then thinking, intellectual work, creativity, memory they are all enhanced because all of these things are in the frontal lobe of the brain and sensory pleasures are all at the back of the brain.

Lord Buddha never said, 'There is no God.' He simply refused to speak on it because in those days there were so many traditions. The Vedic tradition was so alive and there was Jain tradition. There were so many other traditions and people knew it all by books and they could give great talks on peace and meditation but forgot the experience of meditation. So Buddha didn't want to get into controversy like what we do, we don't want to get into any controversy. We have a simple message to say, here is the way to become peaceful. Do this breathing and you will become peaceful.

So similarly, Buddha said, 'I am not going to speak on God but I want to speak about sorrow and there is a way to get rid of sorrow. It is possible to be free from sorrow'. So his focus was very practical and very simple. He spoke on liberation, Moksha which is common to all different sects of Hinduism.

Two and a half thousand years after Krishna's time there was nobody to reform the knowledge, so Buddha came and reformed it. Then later on, Buddhism also became into so many sects. Five hundred years after Buddha, the whole knowledge got misinterpreted, they started making everybody a monk, the whole system started collapsing then Adi Shankara came and he reestablished the knowledge. So that is why it is said time and again whenever people start forgetting the knowledge then Nature brings on the path someone to revive the knowledge and bring people back on the path of light. So this is happening, so whatever Jesus has said that is again the same ancient truth what is said in the Vedas, the trinity, all those things Jesus has said. 'Love is God', is said in the Vedas, in the Upanishads, the same thing Jesus said.

What is most essential is to find the harmony among all the different traditions. Traditions are one side but humanity, spirituality is most important. No Hinduism, Vedic religion, Islam, Christianity, Buddhism nothing is of any good if humanity, human values and spiritual values are missing.

When the thing has already happened then you know whether it was a wishful thinking or an intuition. Time will tell you whether it was wishful thinking or intuition. There is no definite criterion to know. Yes! Wishful thinking is motivated by desire whereas intuition just happens.

Spirituality joins everything. Different beliefs are there like somebody may be Vaishnav, somebody may be Hindu, somebody may be Christian, but spirituality is experience. I often say, 'Religion is like a banana peel and spirituality is the fruit inside.

You have already assumed that you have all this. Now imagine what the case would be if you had never done meditation. These emotions were happening in you earlier also, and these are happening now as well. But now these lose their grip on you very quickly. Maybe,

a few more advanced courses and you find that you are out of the grip of these emotions.

Don't assume that you have all these negative emotions in you. If you assume this, the same will start manifesting. Where are these emotions right now? You are pure in the present moment. Have faith in your innocence in the present moment. Gradually, you will experience that all these are not present in you, and you would start feeling how beautiful you are from inside. You have heard this earlier, but now you would experience it.

The Guru is not a physical entity, but the Guru is the embodiment of knowledge and discretion. The Guru is pure consciousness. There is no difference between universal consciousness, The Guru and the Self. You should also be a Guru to someone. What does it mean to be a Guru? You don't expect anything from him/her, and do whatever you can to uplift him/her with the feeling of love. Start with the one, then two, three… ten. 'I am for you; you don't need to worry' – Then you would also be able to say this for everybody.

If you suppress lust totally, you won't be able to rise high. Also, if you indulge too much in it, then also it is not going to work. Adopt the middle path. You can progress on the path being a family man. Neither you should force celibacy on you nor should you indulge too much in it. If you see the faces of people who visit these night clubs, you will not find even a glimpse of happiness on their faces. It is like sadness and heaviness are dropping out from their faces.

A saint is one whose consciousness is complete. Manifestation follows his words. When such a person speaks, it is not only on the level of the mind. Those words have depth. It is more beneficial to listen to the master's words directly because he is speaking life's experiences only. Experience kindles experience.

We communicate more through our presence. If our presence doesn't have that love, then the words spoken carry no effect. And there is no need for words where presence carries love. Whatever we convey, it is through our whole existence. It is like when a child cries or laughs, it is coming from every cell of his/her body. This is the indication of a yogi – she/he speaks through existence.

Truth cannot be conveyed on the level of the brain.

If you are intelligent, it happens before. And if you are little less intelligent, then it happens afterward. An intelligent person also learns from others' experiences. But this realization is only authentic if you can experience someone's experience as your own. It doesn't carry any value if a beggar says that he has abandoned everything. How can a beggar abandon anything? He has not earned anything at the first place. Also there are some people who do not understand this even after accumulating a lot of money. But this doesn't mean that you should not earn money. If you are too feverish for money thinking that only it can bring you happiness, then either earn money and see yourself, or learn from others' experience.

The purity of Yoga is there when your intention is clear, you are here to serve. If you count that there are twenty people and I will get this much money, if you think that then it can spoil the purity. That is why we have kept our courses in such a way that the teacher gets a very little amount to cover whatever expenses are there. You know you are doing it as a service and you are keeping a charge because without any charges people don't value it and, of course, you need some finances to make arrangements like the durries and the microphone and all this stuff. So, if your intention is pure, if you are financially and otherwise okay and this is only an added support or income to you then it is okay but if you are thinking only on these lines that I want to make money out of teaching yoga then your whole attitude is changed.

Just imagine a school teacher is teaching the children only to get money and not to see that the students are passing or they should get better. A teacher comes for tuition for an hour and he keeps looking

at the watch then within fifteen minutes he runs away, what is the quality of such a teacher. So there is no individual, personal attention that is given, so if the commercial thing doesn't enter your mind then you are there for the cause, you are there for others.

See wanting happiness is natural, everyone wants happiness but happiness does not come alone. Happiness brings along its twin sorrow also, but no one likes sorrow and everyone wants freedom from sorrow. But what does one want freedom from? Sorrow and to want freedom from sorrow also is natural. Just as much as wanting happiness is natural; the same way, wanting freedom from sorrow is also natural. Okay, now the faster one realizes that happiness is there but sorrow is also there then the desire for freedom becomes stronger.

The one who does not wish for happiness receives freedom and the one who does not even wish for freedom is the one who receives devotion.

One who does not crave for happiness is already free, but if one craves for happiness then one will also crave for freedom. When happiness does not please you then you have achieved freedom, but when freedom also does not please you then you receive DEVOTION!

Devotion brings so much happiness and pleasure to you.

The one you are in love with is fearful. Okay! That we don't know how much you have scared him that he has become so fearful. First, see whether the person you are in love with is also in love with you.

See, sometimes we think we love someone but we don't even know how to express our love properly to another. It is very hard to express how much love you are feeling in your heart to someone else. How are you going to express? With words you will not be able to express. Something as deep as love does not come in the realm of expression. It is very difficult to express and sometimes when you try very hard and with a lot of effort to express this love people get scared. The other person should also know how to accept and receive your love, isn't it? That's why it is important to know how to express and how much of our love to express to each person, yeah!

Just imagine you have someone day and night calling you again and again and telling you, 'I love you, I love you, I love you,' then what you will say, 'Okay, yes, you love me, fine what next, right?'

So until we turn towards wisdom we are not able to express or receive love properly, for that also there is some eligibility. With wisdom one is so full of love that love exudes from every action. In life, when we embrace the divinity then our entire relationships blossom by him/herselves but if you try to fix your relationships one by one it does not work. From one side, things will get better and from the other side, it will get worse, so you be centred in yourself, be in devotion and everything else will be taken care of.

Impressions in the soul bind it to the body. That is what is called Karma.

Boredom! What do you do when you get bored of everything? Let me think what you can do.

This is because you are thinking only about yourself. When you don't know what pleasure you will get you get bored because this world cannot really give you satisfaction, it can only bore you but if you come from a place of giving and not getting then you won't be bored. You will think what I can do, how I can be of great use. If you think on those lines and dedicate your life for a cause then boredom does not arise but if you are seeking joy in action then you will get bored. In simple words, what is boredom?

You are seeking joy in action which you didn't get. You are seeking for some joy in the world which you didn't get and then you got bored. In the beginning, it gave you some happiness, a particular object or situation but when you kept repeating it you got bored. So stop seeking joy in activity know that you are joy and then you won't look for joy and get disappointed or get bored, yeah!

Do your 100% and relax and when you feel that you can do a little better or a little more that indicates that you have been responsible. When you feel you are doing everything that you can then the responsibility shifts away from you.

When you are losing motivation that is a sign that you are tired, you need recuperation. You have said that prana is low. So for one, two or three days go into retreat. Some silence, meditation, yoga, pranayama and a liquid diet will help.

You know sometimes when we eat too much and too much of the wrong food then also you feel so tired, isn't it? How many of you have had this experience? Because when you are not feeling good you eat more and when you eat more you feel even more tired, so it is a catch-22 situation, right? It's a cycle that goes on. So, little detoxification/fresh fruit or juice diet coupled with pranayama will work magic.

When you have no motivation to do anything you feel so lazy to do breathing exercises even, that is why I would advise you to go on a diet and after 1 to 2 days this cleansing would help you.

☐

Understanding the Importance of Seva

Suppose you are stranded in some place and you need someone to give you a lift in his car or taxi and nobody stops his/her car to give you a lift, how would you feel?

You are carrying two bags and you have to go to the restroom in a railway station. You can't leave the bags unattended and you have to go to the restroom, what will you do? You will find some nice elderly person, go to him/her and keep the bags with him/her requesting him/her to take care while you go for five minutes to the restroom. Don't you need others' help? If they refuse to help you then how can you survive? You know in this world as human beings we have to help one another and that is what seva is.

Seva means what? 'Sa' means 'him' which refers to God and 'Eva' means 'like him'; doing things like Him. God does so many things for you but does not expect anything in return from you. Whether you pray to Him, thank Him or not He will still continue to do. He is not doing you a favour. When you thank God, that is for your own joy, it does not matter to God. In the same way, whether people acknowledge your work or not, whether they thank you or not you still do it because you find that it is important to do!

There are two levels, like the molecular level on the basis of which everything is the same. For example, if you see this stand is wood, this door is wood, everything is made from wood, but you cannot sit on the door and neither can you make a chair a door, even though everything is wood. Just like that on one level we say that everything is happening but on another level we are also required to act. You continue to act and as you continue doing you will see that,

'I didn't do anything, everything happened and is happening', that is wisdom.

Once I went to the prison to address the prisoners. I was called to speak to him/her after they had completed the course. So I asked him/her how many of you had committed any crime. No one raised his hand. Then I asked how many of him/her were innocent and had been put into prison, and everyone raised his hand. 'We are innocent, we have not done anything and we have just been put into prison. We have not done anything but it just happened.' So even a thief is saying that he did not do anything but it just happened. A man has murdered another person but when I asked him he said I did not do it, I don't know at that time what went into me that the murder just happened. So a person who has committed some of the worst crimes also says that he did not do it. Just like that people who do wonderful work, if you ask him/her 'Did you do this? they will say, 'No, I didn't do anything; it all just happened, fell into place, I didn't do anything.'

This is a state of consciousness where you realize things are not happening because of your effort; it is happening due to some law, due to some power in the creation which is making everything happen.

Someone blames, you get caught up in this blame game. You stand up and say – I have the master key and I know which button to press and how people will react and how things would change. You should have this confidence – the soul, the spirit in you is the master key. It can turn around the situation, the way you want it. You should have that faith. It may not happen five times but sixth time it will happen. It all depends on your conviction and persistence.

See even if the present is painful it is better to be just with it and finish it, otherwise you are just sweeping it under the carpet. Living in an imaginary world and not realizing the current reality, yeah. So it is better to live it and go through it.

There is a story of Mullah Nasirudin. His wife was pregnant and the time of delivery had come. But the baby was not coming out. When the doctor told this to Mullah Nasirudin, he ran to the market, bought a toy, and kept that toy in front of her wife. He said, 'After all this is my child, so he will surely come out with greed.' Thoughtout our whole life we keep on running behind things with the hope of getting something. We keep on looking for some kind of profit. How would such a person experience happiness? Neither does a greedy person get happiness nor does a person who is bombarded with too many desires. The one who relaxes in his consciousness is happy. One, who is centred, experiences the true happiness. I am not saying there is no happiness in the outer world, but the happiness you get when you go within is incomparable. The world is running in search of happiness. The body gets baked, the mind gets baked, the intellect gets deluded but still we keep on getting stuck in the same repetitive cycle. When you meet Guru, you come to know that you are the source of happiness. Then the mind calms down, and you realize that you are the one in whose search you kept on running here and there.

This is one of the five secrets – the secret of birth. Nature has been very kind that birth has been kept as a secret. Otherwise, you would be living a miserable life remembering all previous incidents that happened in the past lives. But a time will come in your life when your mind would be completely established in the present moment, memory would awake, and you will remember what you were and who you were in your previous births. It is all right if it does not happen with some people.

The whole world is made up of cause and effect. If somebody is rich, that has a reason. If somebody is poor, that also has a reason. But does that mean we don't have any independence of Karma? You definitely have freedom. We have been given discrimination. So, we do have the freedom of karma, and also we are bearing fruits of past actions as well. It is like you get some capital from someone. Now, it is up to you what you want to do with it. A poor man can become

rich, and a rich can become poor. There are all possibilities. Your karma decided where you were born. But it depends on you where you want to reach.

Acharya gives knowledge, and a Guru gives diksha. Diksha means the height of awareness and intelligence, and not information. A Guru does not simply stuff you with knowledge, but he kindles life force in you. What happens in a Guru's presence? You become more alive. Every cell in your body becomes more alive. A Guru invokes and awakes the intelligence, not just the intellect. The pinnacle of intellect is intelligence.

The Mind is connected with the moon, and the full moon is a symbol of completion, celebration, or pinnacle. Guru Poornima is the day when the disciple wakes up in his/her fullness. And in that fullness, the disciple can't be but grateful. That gratefulness is not that of you and me, dvaita (Duality). But it is of advaita (Non-duality). It is not the river moving to another river, but it is an ocean moving within itself. Both a river and an ocean move. A river moves from somewhere to somewhere. But where does an ocean move to? It moves within itself. And Guru Poornima symbolizes the fullness of the student, of the disciple. The disciple celebrates in gratitude.

There are two schools of thought. One is you visualize dream and work for it. Other school of thought says surrender everything to God, whatever God gives you is the best, and God will take care of everything for you. Where is the compatibility? They appear to be completely opposite. One is your own visualization, your own dream and your perseverance, and another is having trust in God and leaving everything on God. They appear to be incompatible but I would say they are very much compatible.

□

The Five Layers of Our body

We all have five bodies. Our first body is our environment. If there is poison in the environment, this physical body cannot exist. That is called Annarasmaya kosha. Food is not only that you eat. Environment is also food. Air is food for our lungs. Water is also food. Heat or warmth is also a kind of food. If you are in a place where temperature is -40 degrees centigrade, then no matter how much food you have but you won't be able to exist. So, heat is food for our body. One, of course, is the food that we eat. Peace and joy are food for the soul. Our environment is our first body.

Second is Pranamaya kosha – the energy, life force. You can sense when energy is low and when energy is high. You go to a place where there is low energy, and you feel like running away. You go to a place of high energy, and you feel like staying there. How many of you had this experience?

You can feel the effect of eating fresh food and frozen food in your body. Fresh food has more prana, and frozen food has very little prana. Similarly, you find a difference in eating fresh vegetables, and eating thoroughly baked and cooked vegetables. So, second is Pranamaya kosha.

Then is breath. You can nourish your body but if your body is not breathing, it will go under the earth or become ashes. Our physical body has value because of prana, because you are breathing. 90 per cent of impurities in the body go out through the breath. Only 10 per cent impurities are eliminated through urine, stool and sweat.

Then next is mind – Manmaya kosha, the thoughts in the mind. Are you aware of the thoughts happening in your mind?

Then comes Vigyanmaya kosha – Intuitive awareness or knowledge. That is the fourth sheet of our body.

The fifth is the bliss. So these are the five levels of body that one exhibits.

The purpose of religion is to unite people and unite towards God. Horizontal unity towards people and vertical unity to the universal spirit, to God. If any one of these aims is not achieved then we have failed religion; religion has not failed us. We have done discredit, we are discrediting religion. So it's our responsibility, the people's responsibility to see that there is a horizontal unity. That is unity with all the people of the world, as one world and one people. As in the Vedic concept, it is always said 'Vasudeiva kutumbakam' – the whole world is one family. There are different ways of worship. There was only 1 Buddha, there are 32 sects of Buddhism today in India and the world over. There was only 1 Prophet Mohammed and there are 4 or 5 different sects of Islam that is existing; Ahmadia is there, Shia, there is Sunni, and then there is Sufi Islam. Many different types of Islam are there. Similarly there was only 1 Jesus Christ, there are 72 sects of Christianity in the world. In Hinduism, there are countless; so many different philosophies, sects are there. In Jainism, Mahavir was only 1, but after Mahavir there are 5 sects of Jainism which have come into existence. And Sikhism also, there is Nirankari, there is Nihangs, so many, there is Akalis, so many different sects of Sikhism have come. This is the nature of the world. Philosophies grow, different ideas come. But what we should all stick to is the one truth, there is one God, one divinity, and one human race, one human family. This would bring intellectuals together, religious heads together. And then the common people get inspired when both intellectuals, scholars and religious leaders speak the same language of uniting people. Not just uniting people but uniting countries across the globe. Today we cannot afford conflicts, we cannot afford corruption, we cannot afford violence in any form and in society. It's become very dangerous now. So it's high time that we moved towards moral ethical values which forms the basis of any human society. What are ethics? What are the basic ethics? That you don't want someone else to do to you, you shouldn't do to others. This is the ethics. You don't want anybody to obstruct your practice then you should not obstruct others' practice. You don't want to be harmed by anybody, so you should not harm anyone. So these are the basic ethics. Live and let live.

Education, if it lacks value, society gets destroyed. There is unrest in society. So, we need to bring back the values.

We need to reduce stress and tension in people. When stress and tension is gone then there is a hearing that develops in a human being. If you want to listen to others, first you should have a calm mind. If the mind is disturbed, the best of knowledge doesn't enter your mind. You don't receive it, you don't accept it. So a calm and collective mind is essential. And ethics will bring that calm and collective mind. When a top businessman of this country was asked, 'Why didn't you do some unethical business? You could have become very rich very fast.' He said, 'I want to have proper sleep. I want to have good rest, so I don't want to do unethical business and lose my sleep. So, these are the values that we need to inculcate.

India has given this vision of 'Vasudhaiva Kutumbakam' - the world is one family. Many people think Hinduism is a religion of many gods. We worship many gods. That's what people say. I say this is misunderstanding. Like in Islam, there are 99 names to 1 God. Why should God have 99 names, why not 1 name? There is no explanation. God has many attributes so you have 99 names. In Hinduism they say 1008 names. And 1008 names they say it can have any number of forms. But with different forms it is the same being, same divinity, same light. Like one white light when it passes through the prism it splits into 7 colours. These 7 coloured rays are not different from one white light, they are the very expression of this one light. Seven different colours, one God has different attributes. Like Jesus, if you go to a church, you will have one shrine for mercy, another shrine for compassion, another shrine for healing. It's the same Jesus but there are 12 stations in which they present Jesus for

different specific needs or ways of worshipping. Similarly, there is one God – there is one truth. But the learned say He's been called in many names and many forms. So it is not form. God is not in idols. But idol is only to create an atmosphere of serenity. It's said you can have idol, you can have water, you can have fire, you can have tree, you can use any element in the creation to create devotion, to create an atmosphere for you to go deep within to find one God. This is what the Vedic principles are. A Vedic principle is not worshipping other than one God. It is worshipping the same God. But to worship you can use different things, different symbolisms. So this symbolism is very different in different religions. Where people are in conflict is not with the values, not with ethics. People get into conflicts when they just stick onto the symbol. And there is fight between different inter-religious and intra-religious factions. So these sorts of conflicts can be avoided when we move into the true ethics and intellectual basis of all religions. Then it brings people's hearts and minds together and make a more beautiful world. We need to give a better world to our children than what we have inherited.

This is a skill! If there is no feverishness, it happens. Have you seen how a child behaves when he sees chocolates? He eats a couple, then stuffs some in one pocket and tries stuffing more in the other. The child is in a frenzy. An adult does not have this feverishness. When such feverishness for the objects is missing, then only you actually enjoy the object of senses.

You experience, you enjoy, but without craving for it, knowing that the joy comes from within you. The object is only a reflection. When you realize that joy is within and not in the object outside then only you can enjoy.

This is little profound and it clicks to a mature mind.

A terrorist does whatever he does with hatred, with ignorance, right? You cannot take a policeman or an army man and a terrorist as the same. They both shoot with guns, but a policeman does it for a different reason and a terrorist does it for an entirely different reason. The intention, the state of mind is totally different. That is why Arjuna was told, 'Fight the war for justice, but not with anger, hatred, jealousy or greed. Do it to protect the dharma, the righteousness.'

There is a neutral gender as well. There are 3 genders. Some things fall under the neutral gender too. In fact, there is a whole scripture on the gender of stones as well as trees. The Shilpa Shastra or Book on Sculptures elaborates on this. Hawaiians also say that different stones have different genders! They can identify those. But it doesn't matter. The Self, or the Spirit is beyond gender.

On the spiritual path you need to have that zeal and enthusiasm for sacrifice. Just today I met several swamis – all young people – computer engineers and highly qualified people. They've sacrificed their whole career, life, everything to bring education to poor people, to do service in society. They're doing service day and night. They're not wishing anything for him/herselves. They're not thinking, 'Oh, what will happen to me?' They have dedicated their lives to build schools and colleges and to bring education to millions. So, it is necessary for a bigger cause. Sacrifice brings a bigger joy! It doesn't reduce your joy. When our needs are more, our responsibilities are less. When our needs are less, we are able to take up bigger responsibilities. That is the happiest life!

Because you are beautiful too, that's why I appear peaceful to you. If you were not beautiful then you would know nothing about my beauty. Whatever quality you have, only that gets projected onto the world outside. So, what you see in me, take that as your own. If you don't feel beautiful, become beautiful. What is stopping you? Become that.

The whole world is spherical: everything moves in cycles. You

have to come back, but you have a choice. If you are born out of compulsion then it's the same old story again and again. But if you get liberated, then you have the choice and the will to be born when you want. When you come back liberated, it is joyful.

If you have to get angry, get angry at bigger things, not the small usual mundane stuff. Get angry at corruption in the system and injustice happening around you. Give a bigger dimension to your anger and see all the small things become simply insignificant. I want you to go and talk to every youth in this country and in the world. Talk to him/her. Tell him/her to take action against corruption. If the head of the government is shielding corrupt people, what can you do? People have to wake up. That's what we all have to do. Everyone should speak out against corruption.

Life is a combination of both – dynamism and silence, chaos and quietness. You shouldn't be afraid of either. Those who are used to chaos, are scared of silence. Many times, in my public talks I have observed that some people can't even close their eyes, they're so scared. Sometimes politicians and even professors can't sit for 10 minutes with eyes closed. They're scared to do so. People are so scared of silence, of stillness, of closing their own eyes. Similarly, people who are used to their silence, to their comfort zone are so scared of chaos and disturbance. Both are incomplete. You should feel as comfortable with silence as you are with chaos, and that is the art of living. We see dynamism in silence and silence in chaos. When you are at home with both of him/her you are able to contribute in both situations.

Your desire to be free indicates that you're already on the way out. It is already going away. Do not be too hard on yourself. Practices will help you a lot.

Know the impermanence of everything. Okay, you get a desire.

It will be fulfilled. So what? Time will devour all. Time will change everything, so keep moving. When you know everything is impermanent and can still enjoy everything at the same time, that is vairagya or detachment.

Having too many thoughts indicates some weakness in the body. Consult an ayurveda physician and take herbs to cleanse the body. Through pranayama, the mind is purified. Through meditation, the consciousness gets purified. Sometimes the thoughts come because of the surroundings or company. Do not be afraid of bad thoughts. These thoughts are similar to the dark clouds that come and pass away.

This universe is already heaven. What blocks us from perceiving it as heaven is our own mind. The mind clings onto the past or it wants perfection. It has its own ideas of perfection. This is about the universe. But if you ask me about improving the society, I think this is a question every human being should ask himself. I think we need to have a violence-free and stress-free society. The way to such a society is Yoga, Meditation and Service.

The voice of truth needs to be heard louder. You're right. It is time for the revolution. It has to be loud. People should come together. People should stand up for human values. It will happen.

When you have inner satisfaction then everything happens effortlessly for you. When you don't have that, even small things become a struggle. Wisdom is about having that inner satisfaction. Wake up and see what is bothering you and why you are not satisfied. You don't have food, you don't have shelter, you don't have money or you don't have a companion. Pinpoint the area and then deal with it. You think when you have an amount of money or that much fame, then you will be happy. Wake up and see life from a broader perspective and you will see that this is not the truth. This is another illusion.

Then you settle down. Meditation is the answer.

When you are waiting for an answer, what is waiting? The mind has already stopped. When you are astonished, the mind has stopped. When you are in laughter, or panic, or fear, or when you are in deep love, the mind has stopped. Time has stopped. There is an experience of timelessness. Have you experienced that timelessness? Just sit on the banks of the Ganges alone and watch the water flowing. Suddenly you feel it is a moment of eternity. The same way, when you watch the sun rise or set, the moon rise or set or watch a child playing, a sudden spurt of energy comes from within you and the mind is already still. You don't have to wait for this to happen sometime in the future. It is happening here and now.

Have you seen movies? There is a hero and a villain in the movie. Now what is the role of a villain? He creates some kind of entertainment. When do you feel your body is a burden to you? When you feel that your body is a suffering to the spirit. But you can't call it a burden when it is a means to elevate the spirit. When you know the body is given to you as an instrument to elevate the spirit, would you still call it a burden? 'Shareer maadhyam paro dharma sadhna' – This body is an instrument for dharma, all that uplifts the spirit. Don't consider it a burden. Honour your own body. The soul comes to your body after great effort. There is a great rush. Many souls compete to get one body and one succeeds. So our body is a gift, and not a burden.

What is burden? Desires, cravings and aversions in the mind are the burden. Your craving for something or your aversion for something makes you feel it is a burden. Losing your body doesn't make you lose your cravings and aversions.

It is the mind which makes you feel it is a misery. This world is a part of the divinity. So instead of blaming the world, look inside.

When you are open from within, then you can't but love everyone and everyone can't but love you. Neither you have a choice nor does he. You have done this as a baby. Do you remember how you were as a baby? Being natural, simple, innocent, without any barrier and free with everybody.

When someone near to you is leaving the body, your words would have no meaning. At those moments, you just be there in silence. Those vibrations will work for him/her.

As much as you have changed, don't you think others will also change? Nobody knows everything in the world. We all know something. In fact, when you see the magnitude of knowledge, you find it can't be completely known. But aren't you obliged to give others whatever little you know? That is what you have to do. The world doesn't expect you to do service which you are not capable of. The world expects you to do what you can. If you are a doctor then people will run to you in case of an emergency. At that time, your saying no doesn't make sense. And if you are not a doctor and are approached to do something that you can't, you simply say – 'I am sorry. I can't do it.' We do what we can and we ask pardon for what we can't.

Prosperity and spirituality can coexist but greed and spirituality can't coexist. Unethical means of earning money and spirituality simply cannot coexist. If you have a factory or a business, you can continue to do that and still be very ethical. You don't have to leave your industry, which may be giving employment to a few hundred or more people, for spirituality. There is no need for saying materialism is bad and leaving that you want to go towards spirituality. That is not at all necessary. You can continue doing your duty. This is what is expressed in one of the scriptures 'Ashtavakra' where Ashtavakra told king Janaka that he could be a king and be totally spiritual. King

Janaka was the embodiment of the highest knowledge. There are many examples like this. What I usually say is 'keep money in your pocket and not in your heart or head'. When the money is wrongly placed that is when the problem arises. In India, materialism and spirituality are not in conflict with each other. Lakshmi – the symbol of material prosperity – is portrayed pressing the feet of Narayana – the symbol of spirituality. We always say LaxmiNarayana, which refers to the combination of wealth and spirit. But it is very important to note that greed and spirituality don't go together.

Unfortunately we associate negative tendencies like greed and jealousy with materialism. Even if you have to do charity, you can't do it with an empty bowl. How can you think of feeding ten hungry children with no money at hand? Is it not your dharma to feed him/her? In one of the ancient scriptures in India it is said, 'Righteousness comes from wealth'. Proper governance is the basis of the economy. I think it is all connected. And the most important is the faith in the being, the highest self – the faith that: 'I am going to get whatever I need and whenever I need.' Then you give miracle a chance. Materialism is measuring every step too much. (Then you don't know when the stock market is going to crash and banks are going to be bankrupt.) Don't bank your faith on the banks, but bank your faith on the divinity and the power of your own sankalpa (positive sankalapa) and thoughts.

There are three things which are very important whenever you sit for meditation:

1. I want nothing for the next 20 minutes or half an hour.
2. I do nothing.
3. I am nothing.

Any effort is an impediment in meditation and so 'I do nothing'. And then if you have any notions about yourself, I am rich, I am poor, I am intelligent or I am stupid, you can't go into meditation. You cannot progress on the spiritual path. So you have to come to this – I am nothing.

These are the three golden rules which I feel are very important and with which you can sink deep into meditation.

I don't know how much of pranayama and asanas (postures) you can make someone do when he/she is sick and dying. It may not be possible at all. Some good bhajans (uplifting music), soft and instrumental music will also help. This is called laya yoga. Some words of wisdom will help. This is gyan yoga. Your mere presence there will help. Your being there without any effort will help. When we are in the 'doing' consciousness, thinking what to do, we reduce our energy. When we are in the 'being' consciousness, suddenly the light, air and energy come in you. You can make him/her feel better with that presence and energy of yours.

When you do service, you gain merit and that merit helps you to go deep into yourself. So service helps you gain merit, merit takes you deep into sadhna (self-effort and practices) and sadhna makes you come up and do more service. It is all cyclically connected. So, it is not going to be complete if any one aspect is missing.

Service is that which is needed by the people.

Don't regret about the past, however it has been. You have learnt the lesson. Just accept it and move on, learning from it.

Bhakti yoga is seeing the Divine as mine and oneself as belonging to the Divine, and all that exists belongs to the Divine.

If I have a choice I would take away all the definitions and leave you in confusion because from that confusion something flowers up in you. My understanding is not going to help you. It has to come from within you. When you wake up and see, you will be surprised. I would like you to experience that WOW. Don't make it a concept.

If you don't know what enlightenment is, thank God and say, ' I don't know what enlightenment is. Let me wait for it.' It is the concepts that keep us away from experiencing the reality. That's what I feel.

All the lines between different disciplines are blurred now. I remember when I was in school there was a thick line of difference between physics and chemistry, and they were thought not to be connected. Today, whether it is astrophysics, physics, knowledge about the spirit or information technology, all have come together. Environment and spirituality are not two different things. Perhaps the ancient people of this country knew this. They worship trees, mountains, rivers, etc. in Nature. And it is true for all native civilizations in the world. They honoured Nature. They took care that they care for Nature and progress and development was aligned with the sustainable conditions on planet Earth. The most needed thing today is – Globalizing wisdom. There are two types of calamities – one is natural calamities like earthquakes. And second is a man-made calamity. Man-made calamities can be overcome by wisdom and a Cultural Revolution, and by spreading this knowledge of a one-world family. We are anyway one. There is no two.

Natural calamities can be overcome by caring for the planet, planting more trees, preserving water, by spiritual energy and with the thought that you are one with the vishavatma (Universal soul). An intention or thought that you are one with vishavatma and a little attention manifests itself.

From the Indian perspective sin is that which brings misery to many and merit is that which brings love, happiness and joy to many. Sin is something that could be washed out. It is not your nature. If sin is your very nature, you can never get rid of it. Like if mud is your skin, you cannot get rid of it. But if it is on your skin you can take a dip and it will get washed away. If the flaw is inside the diamond, it can't be corrected. But if slush is on the diamond, it just needs a little water to be poured on and it gets clean.

Here in India, we consider sin as a superimposition. There are

three things in Yoga – Malah, Avarna and Vikshepa. Malah is impurities in the body, vikshepa is impurity on the mind, restlessness and disturbances in the mind and avarana is the sheath which covers the spirit, which is the ego-identification with one little thing. And the purpose of Yoga is to cleanse the three sheaths of impurity. Yoga loosens up all the three sheaths of impurities. And then the true spirit which is part of the divinity shines through.

So I don't consider sin is your nature but sin is that which you have acquired due to ignorance. And with the light of knowledge it just disappears.

A part of the consciousness is all pervading and a part remains. It is like the air in the balloon; it is trapped in the impressions, and then it comes back.

Don't do too much of practice. Move ahead gradually. Do only as much as needed. Do that much to which your body gets accustomed to. You should not start doing 10 hours of practice all of a sudden.

Experience happens on its own. Don't hanker for experiences.

Ego is feeling uncomfortable in the presence of someone else. Self-confidence is, feeling at home. Being natural is antidote to ego, and being natural is so complementary to confidence. It goes with confidence and is inseparable from confidence. When you are confident, you are natural. If you are natural, you are confident

This 'always' is the problem. Don't try to hold onto the 'always'. Take life as it comes. So what if all those clouds come for a moment. Your nature never goes and your nature is love. That cannot be changed.

You take it with a pinch of salt. Sometimes because of your own impressions, your own desires, or own fears, you have those

visions. So, you cannot trust your vision 100 per cent till you are totally hollow and empty.

Mind means moods, thoughts, opinions, ideas, all these things that we collect. And, no mind is meditation. Dawn and dusk are considered very good for meditation. So, whenever you meditate, or whenever the bad time is there, you meditate. When you meditate you go off the influence of the mind and go into the self. The self is Shiva tattva. Shiva tattva means always benevolent, caring, loving, uplifting. That consciousness deep within you which is caring, loving, uplifting and benevolent will nullify the negative influences of the mind and the time.

□

Understanding the Play of Colours

Life should be full of colours! And each colour is meant to be seen and enjoyed separately, for if seen all mixed together, they will appear all black. All the colours like red, yellow, green, etc. should exist side by side and simultaneously be enjoyed together.

Similarly, in life, different roles played by the same person should exist peacefully and distinctly inside him. For example, when a father continues to play his role of a 'father' in office, things are bound to go for a toss. In our country, a politician is sometimes a father first and a leader later!

In whichever situation we are in, we should play the corresponding role to the hilt and then life is bound to become colourful! This concept was called 'Varnashram' in ancient India. This meant – everyone, be it a doctor, teacher, father, whoever or whatever, is expected to play his/her role with full enthusiasm. Mixing professions will always be counter productive. If a doctor wants to do business, he should run a business separately and secondary to his profession and not make business out of medicine. Keeping these 'containers' of the mind separate and distinct is the secret of a happy life and this is what HOLI teaches.

All colours emanate from white, and when mixed again, they become black. When your mind is white and consciousness – pure, peaceful, happy and meditative, different colours and roles emerge. We get the strength to play various roles with full sincerity against the background. We have to dip into our consciousness time and again. If we only look inwards and play around with colours outside of us, we are bound to find blackness all over again. Between roles we have to take deep rests, in order to play each role sincerely. Now, the biggest impediment to deep rest is desire. Desire means stress.

Even petty desires cause high stress – the higher goals give relatively less botheration! Desire tortures the mind at times.

So, what does one do?

The only way out is to focus attention on the desire and surrender it. This act of focusing awareness or sight on the desire or Kama is called 'Kamakshi'. With awareness, desire loses its grip and surrender happens and then nectar flows out from within. Goddess Kamakshi holds a sugarcane stem in one hand and a flower in the other. The sugar-cane stem is so hard and has to be squeezed in order to obtain sweetness, while the flower is soft and collecting nectar from it is so easy. This truly represents life, which indeed has a little of both! It is far easier to obtain this bliss from the inside than it is to try to extract pleasure from the outside world – which needs a lot more effort.

Lift your spirit with the joy of colour!

The long hair is like an antenna to receive messages from God and the long beard is like an earthing to transmit those messages to the people.

We must make you sit in a closed small room and play loudspeaker 24 hr. And not some good music, some heavy music. Then after 24 hours, when we switch it off you will come to know what sitence is.

The test of your peace is only when there are obstacles. Be thankful to obstacles.

God cannot see two. For God, there is no you and I! He can only see Himself in everything and everyone!

Scepticism is perfectly all right, but not cynicism. That drains your energy. One can be sceptical to begin one's journey and I would

very much appreciate and welcome that. Because you would have gone through scepticism, the faith will be strongly built.

Dispassion starts happening naturally. When you grow up, your mind doesn't get stuck to small things like lollipop, yet when you reached school or college that attachment naturally dropped. Similarly, with toys or even friends. When you grow up, you still have friends but you rise above that entanglement. Naturally entanglement starts leaving you. If dispassion doesn't happen then you experience sorrow.

When the value of dharma is missing then there is suffering in the world. It's because we have forgotten the values of life. When adharma took over, when people forgot the real essence of dharma, Bhagwan Buddha came to re-establish dharma. The message He spread was 'Ahimsa Parmo Dharma'.

Meditation means you do not feel the time. You get connected with the Universal Spirit.

October 2 is remembered as a day of Non-Violence to mark Mahatma Gandhi's birthday. Mahatma Gandhi is synonymous with non-violence and truth. In today's times, we see so much domestic violence, societal violence, tension and depression that it's appropriate to honour October 2 as Non-Violence Day. Every day should, in fact, be a non-violence day and that is the art of living. Every day should be a celebration and when there is celebration there is no violence.

First, you think you are bound, and then you try to come out of that. You find freedom when you have a say over your emotions and when you are in wisdom.

Nobody is completely independent. Even nations are not

completely independent. The word is interdependent. Among nations and communities we are interdependent. We live in an interdependent world. Man depends on woman and a woman has to depend on man.

So it is paradox – independence and interdependence. Try to be independent as much as you can, understanding the need for interdependency.

Everyone has both female and male genes. You are made up of both your father and mother – Half father and half mother. Divinity is both male and female. This was acknowledged long ago and represented as Ardhnareeshwar. God is neither just man, nor just woman. He is Ardhnareeshwar – Whole creation is both male and female.

Goddess Durga is the mother, so sweet and compassionate, and She is riding on Tiger – most ferocious. Completely opposite! Opposite values are complementary and ancient people recognized this. Scientifically, the whole creation cannot sustain even if one animal goes missing. Each of these animals brings down to the earth a bio-energy corresponding to a particular wavelength. A tiger carries the vibration of goddess Durga.

Goddess Saraswati has so many hands! In one hand, she carries a rosary – rosary represents meditation, in another she carries a book – intellectual knowledge and with the other she plays a musical instrument – Veena. Only when intellectual knowledge, music and meditation come together, then wisdom dawns. This complete knowledge was there even several million years ago. Saraswati sits on a rock meaning once you have acquired wisdom, it is deeply grounded in you. Goddess Laxmi sits on a lotus meaning money is flowing – any time anything can happen. Wealth moves and it should move.

You can feel you are a mother to the whole world. Being a mother is in the very nature of a woman. That compassion, that love and caring will be there.

Whether a woman should marry or not, that is her decision. Most important is to be happy. That is my opinion. There are many who are single and happy, and there are many who are married and not happy, and vice versa! Choice is yours, blessings are mine.

Whatever you want to learn, you can do it on the Internet. Such a glorious age – one laptop and that is it. Google it and anything on earth is available! Knowledge at the tips of the finger. I used to say that knowledge will be at the tips of your fingers. I didn't understand why was I saying it and neither did those who heard me. All the information, not knowledge is there.

Even demons ask for boons from her and angels as well. Once somebody was telling this joke: Once a man was asked who the owner of the house was. The man replied saying he would ask his wife!

□

The Traits to Achieve Goals

First is fixing the goal itself. The mind is so wavering – so getting the goal fixed is most important. Then you have to fix the time-frame. Then weighing the consequences – adverse and favourable and then your ability to adapt to changes. Ability to adopt the means to achieve the goals is important.

Spirituality is the same for men and women. At some time in history, men put certain bans so that women might not rise in power. But there are certain norms of society and one should adhere to that.

You are planning now what to do in the future to be in the present moment! Got it?

Yes, communism says equal opportunity for everyone. Spirituality says Divine is in every heart and so all are unique. That way both talk of the same thing.

You can have the same feeling, but the expression will have to be different. You express love differently towards the elderly and with kids you are different. Love is the same but the way you express it is different.

Know that no mistake can be corrected with anger. Only with awareness can anything be corrected.

You know, the world once was a beautiful place to live in where all would celebrate diversity. But what happened that caused so much division? I would want all to rise above the differences and move ahead. Whatever your attitude is from the outside, but have that naturalness from inside. Have the skill to create belongingness with all.

Divine principle is not someone in the sky. It is inside you in the form of consciousness!

Every instant we are getting something to learn from the whole world. All that is needed is awareness!

Each individual is a beautiful scripture designed by God. Study your own mind and then observe the minds of people around. What do we do? We don't observe our own mind but we keep on wasting efforts in judging others' minds. First, understand your own mind and then you will be able to understand what's happening in the big mind, in the minds of all.

You know, whomsoever I meet in the world, I feel that belongingness. I never feel I am meeting someone for the first time. So many times we have come to this World. I know a little bit, but you have forgotten. Keep smiling this time.

When you think good of yourself, you think ill of others; and when you think others' are good, you think you are not OK. Such complexes are there in many children, today. So the attitude that neither I am bad, nor anybody else is bad gives such a sense of acceptance of everybody and your own self. Sadhana enables one deprogram all past programming.

Bliss comes out of chaos and the ability to enjoy chaos is enlightenment.

Sometimes people say words and they really don't feel that way. Don't you do it sometimes? As children, you say things that you

don't really mean. Kids usually say things they mean. As we grow older, our feelings and words grow apart. They are not the same. Now, don't worry about what other people are feeling. Feelings are fleeting. One day they feel good, next day they don't. Don't bother about this. Simply acknowledge that that person is not feeling good and that he/she is here to work on it. Our being angry that someone is feeling bad doesn't make sense. Sometimes their feelings change but your feelings remain the same. Someone puts a doubt in your mind and then he/she forget but you hold on to it. The same is with senior citizens who complain but then forget while you hold on to the complaint.

GDP of a country should be now measured with GDH- Gross Domestic Happiness. Factor which state is happy, which country is happier than the other. Having a big bank balance and being depressed is not prosperity. You should have the mind to enjoy that prosperity. You may have enough food, but you suffer from diabetes and depression and heart problem. That doesn't count to be a healthy society. So whether it is economy or politics, social entrepreneurship or any activity, everything is centred around one fact – welfare of the society.

Look at the present moment – now, now, now! Wake up NOW! Everything else is stupid. All that has happened has gone into emptiness. Everything dissolves into emptiness. Your entire past – wiped out! All the things that you felt are gone. Good or bad, they are gone. So, wake up to the truth of the present moment. Divinity is in the present moment. This is yoga. Yoga is being established in the moment. And moment does not mean fleeting moment. The moment has the depth of infinity; it has all the past and all the future.

Who cares what you feel? Throw your feelings into the ocean. A little sensation or discomfort arises. Who cares? Are you doing what you want to do? And, in doing what you want to do, are you keeping the delicacy of your consciousness or are you being like a bulldozer (I will do whatever I want)? Being like a bulldozer is being insensitive. Both being oversensitive and very weak and being like a bulldozer are not correct. The best combination is being sensitive and strong. This is wisdom and this is what we have to work on.

The effect of past actions is limited. Past actions definitely affect you, e.g. you drive fast, get a ticket, and you have to pay. Get three tickets and you have to surrender your licence, no doubt. But don't brood over it. Wake up. When you wake up, even the consequences you fear will not happen. You will be forgiven in that moment. The moment we acknowledge our mistake, we are forgiven. So you are innocent every moment you are awake. Now! Now! Now!

Take the challenge. Whenever someone is nasty towards you, do something so nice that it takes him by surprise. You will suddenly find there is a shift happening. If it does not happen also, it is fine. At least, you have done something good.

The world is a very funny place, I tell you. Either it is very entertaining or it is such a pain and so miserable! You can't take it. Sometimes, you do so much for someone and he turns his back and does things that harm you. Many parents say, 'We did so much for my children and now they are dissociating from us.' Not just with parents, but the same with employers, friends, siblings, and even spouses. Speaking of a spouse, there are four stages of marriage. The first stage is mad for each other. The second stage is made for each other. The third stage is mad at each other. The fourth stage is mad because of each other.

Just be natural. When prayer is happening, don't create a conflict and confusion in yourself. Don't say, 'Oh, it will happen anyway!' But prayer does not have to happen by compulsion.

All the sensory nerves end in the tip of the nose. There are two points that are important for alertness and focus of the brain – the ear lobes and tip of the nose. They are the marma points. These are the secret points. If you keep your attention on the tip of the nose, your focus improves, especially for children. In the Jain tradition, they can multiply 100 numbers (avadhan). They focus on the tip of the nose. It's amazing! They are faster than computers. Shathavadhanis, as they are called. Avadhan is the technique of holding memories in your consciousness. It is like a photographic memory. People who follow this technique, Avadhanis, can tell you what date was Tuesday in 1700. This knowledge was systematically erased. That is the unfortunate part.

Ayurveda is a complete science. It describes dincharaya (daily routine) and ritucharya (seasonal routine). Dinacharya includes meditation for the balancing of the three doshas (mind or body type). The mind has an impact on the body and all its doshas and gunas (three qualities of nature: sattva, rajas and tamas). So, the mind, breath, herbs – they are all linked. Similarly, ayurveda helps one to meditate deeply. Too many thoughts indicate high pitta (one of the three doshas). So pitta must be treated. In ayurveda, combinations are referred to as 'yoga'. For example, when two herbs are put together, it is called yoga. So that concept of yoga is similar to meditation and to ayurveda.

Don't limit our relationship. Let love be love, don't give it a name. For a master, no disciples exist. But for a disciple, the Master exists. See, if you do the Kriya, you are initiated.

When you recognize that this is your pattern, wake up and say, 'I will not be a victim of this pattern!' You have that strength! You will be given that strength.

'Pradosha' is the time when divine energy dawns on the planet and redeems all the spirits. There are so many spirits. For people who die and exist as spirits, the day of pradosha redeems him/her, frees him/her, freedom not just for the spirits but also for human beings. Desires are fulfilled and the mind gets cleared. Shivaratri that comes once a year, known as 'Maha Shivaratri', is very special, the great night of Lord Shiva.

□

Understanding the Space Within

I'm going to talk to you about another dimension of space, that is, the inner space – the space that rules your life, the space from which all thoughts and emotions emerge, of which you are simply a puppet. There may be rules, but when your emotions rise high, you become a victim of your own emotions. If your thought patterns are prejudiced, are caught up in some utopian or nasty concepts then you behave that way.

The difficulty with human beings, normal human beings is that we seldom take time to look at our own emotions, look at our own thought patterns, at what's happened inside. We act before thinking; we act before even resolving our feelings. So when the feelings override your actions, your concepts and prejudices override your action; time to time crimes are bound to happen in society, whatever rules are there.

Inner rules are just like the watchman, the doorkeeper, but the emotions are the owner of the home. So when the owner barges in, the doorkeeper just gives way. And this is exactly what happens. If you just talk to any criminal anywhere he will either justify his action or feel completely helpless, because he feels he himself is the victim. So I often say, 'Inside every culprit is a victim crying for help.' If we attend to the victim, the culprit disappears. And this is exactly what we need to do, whether it's the crime that's being done either in Kosovo and Serbia or Bosnia or Sri Lanka or anywhere. It's the people who do that, and 'normal people', as the honourable speaker mentioned just a few minutes ago. They're normal people, but what makes normal people do abnormal crimes is the lack of education about their emotions.

Neither at home nor at school are any of us taught how to manage

our greed, our anger, our jealousy, our frustration and our rage. Nobody teaches you how to manage this mind by which we do all our actions. We don't have to go to outer space to feel that the earth is very small, that we all belong to one another. We can wake up here when we attend to our inner space.

Find out, observe, that whatever I am, everybody else is. So, we are all one, we are all part of one human family, human species. This awareness, this awakening has to happen within each one of us, within each individual on the planet and this is where individual education will lead to a collective culture. A culture in the society, it's all an individual who forms the unit of a culture. So, it's the individual who forms the unit of a society. So if individuals are educated, we have a literate society. There's nothing like a society that can become literate; literacy has to happen through individuals. And similarly, education in handling oneself knowing oneself has to happen individually and that will have to lead to a collective phenomenon called a civilized, cultured society.

It's superstitions, dogmas, prejudices that overrule our civilization today. You know what happened in the Middle Ages, in the Medieval period, either in the Spanish Inquisition or the witch hunting, in the name of some dogmas, or the caste system in the East. They all have proved to be disasters, a disaster to society, and education will make people overcome these ills. Similarly, corruption, what we are facing in the business community today – sort of low morals and somehow we're lost…we don't know what to do. So in these situations, an introspection and understanding about human nature, the nature of mind, the nature of our emotions, and in a large spectrum, the purpose of life.

As somebody recently said, that the GDP of a country should be now measured with GDH, Gross Domestic Happiness factor. You should see which state is happy, which country is happier than the other. Having a big bank balance and being depressed for the whole life is not prosperity. You should have the mind to enjoy that prosperity. You may have enough food and enough things to eat, but you suffer from diabetes and depression and heart problem. That doesn't count to be a healthy society. So whether it is economy or politics, social

entrepreneurship or any activity, everything is centred around one fact: welfare of the society, that is, wellness of the society. If the wellness is at stake no other factor will suffice for the society to be uplifted. So we need to look into that.

And ethics form one of the backbones of wellness and business forms its wings. Without business, wellness cannot happen. So, we need to consider this. I'm happy that we're all on the same page here, but from very different fields, pondering on something that would make a breakthrough in the crisis of today. □

The Need for Ethical Practices

2000 years ago the great acharya Kautilya had said that the basis of ethics is economy, the basis of economy is state and the basis of state is civil society. If the civil society is not following ethics, the state can't do anything about it.

And civil society has to follow ethics.

What can uplift the society?

Usually the youth are of the opinion that you can't succeed if you are not unethical. Now, people are becoming more aware after the crisis.

In Chinese, the same word means crisis and opportunity. Recently, a prominent businessman in India was asked, 'Why doesn't he take bribes?' He replied, 'He wants good sleep.' What people are looking for is an example. Many people can describe crisis, but only a few can turn it around. Good ethics give good sleep and good profit.

Ethical practices are essential for a good economy. We need to come up with practical solutions. 90 per cent of the population is honest! People are waiting for examples and support.

We need to caution people without creating fear and anxiety. Spiritual values can reinstate faith in humans.

Everyone has needs and responsibilities. See how we can reduce our needs and increase the responsibilities. This is absolutely essential in today's world. When the equation between needs and responsibility is disturbed, then we have chaos.

In Hyderabad, a group of our people refused to give bribe for getting license for their business. They said, 'We are willing to come 50 times; we respect you but we cannot give bribe.' It completely transformed the mindset of the people. The group received 10 licenses. Young people, young blood can transform the way business is practised.

We need to set examples among the state and stakeholders. □

Understanding Nirvana

Nirvana is bringing the balance and having no feverishness for any desire. Desire means a lack. When you say, I want nothing, I am content, that is nirvana. But that doesn't mean you shun your duties. You perform your duties well but you are with your centre. Even craving for enlightenment is an hindrance to enlightenment.

All emotions are linked with people, objects and events. Catching onto objects, people or relationships hinders freedom, liberation. When the mind is free from all impressions and concepts, you are liberated. The state of nothingness is called Nirvana, enlightenment, Samadhi. Nirvana is getting back to me from mine. Who am I?

When you go deep inside you, layer after layer, that is nirvana. It is like peeling an onion! What do you find in the centre of an onion? Nothing!

When you know that everything is changing – all relationships, people, body, feelings – suddenly the mind which clings onto misery comes back to you. The return from mine to me gives you contentment and freedom from misery. Reposing in that state of contentment is nirvana.

When you forgive then your mind becomes calm. Tell him/her with compassion and love, not with anger. If you become happy by putting guilt in someone's mind that is not good either. Tell him/her with love and then you drop it.

Life without joy,
Heart without compassion,
Mind without imagination,

And Intellect without intuition is incomplete.

Life is all celebration. Celebration happens when all come together, and a society without celebration is no good.

Divine love is not somewhere far, it is with me right here. If we have this faith then we can never feel separate from Divine love. I have come to tell you that you can never be far from God. If you understand this today then I will consider my work done.

Devi and Devtas are the different forms of God. Honour him/her and rest deep in your subtle Self.

Is there only one type of sweet, then how can God be of one kind? Yesterday 5,600 types of dishes were displayed. 35,000 children, who had never seen these many varieties of sweets, ate from the spread.

A few years ago, an event called Brahma Naad was organized in Delhi where 1,200 sitarists performed.

People said it's not possible. Yet, to make the impossible possible is our work. In Pune, 2,700 vocalists came together. Then the Gujarat team came up with this idea of Annam Brahm.

Just know that whatever you want, you will get.

Lord Krishna said, 'Leave all religions and come to Me; I will liberate you from all your sins.' But we do just the opposite. We keep clinging to our religions and start our journey to save ourselves from our own sins.

In the rush of our daily lives, we forget that Divinity is within us. Let us all take this sankalpa – Remembering again and again that the Divine music is within us, my family and I take this commitment that people all over the world should stay happy.

We are part of a Smashta Jeevan – An individual human being is connected to the whole universe, with all its life forms. Birds, animals and the life of people should be respected. When we care for Nature, Nature cares for us. It makes us complete and completeness is the basis of a human being. We need to take care of plants and animals. One of the most divine expressions is to plant a tree. Then we need to take care of people. Ladies while cooking should take out one handful of grains every day or once a week or once a month and feed the poor. It is said that two to three hundred years back, there was not even one poor or hungry person in India. Such a complete and capable country we had.

Once again, we must resurrect this country to that state. We should all work towards this.

It is said in all our Upanishads that Food is Brahma, and one should honour it. Like they say 'Jaisa ann vaisa mann' – The state of your mind depends on your diet. Pure vegetarian food keeps our mind perfect, intellect sharp and body fit. That is why many scientists today are switching to vegetarianism.

We offer prayers before eating. The food that we eat absorbs the vibrations. Respecting food means respecting farmers, we should always keep in mind that the one who is producing food should always be happy, because that is the origin of the thought cycle. This is our beautiful tradition, with such deep science behind. Food makes us experience the chaitanya (the consciousness), that is why it is called Brahman.

India is famous for its contribution in seven spheres. First, is the variety of clothing available. Then is the huge variety of food. After this, comes Nritya and Sangeet (Dance and Music) – India is being recognized in these fields as well. Then comes tourism – Pravaas Udhyog, and the I.T Industry, and of course India is making its name in the field of Spirituality – Knowledge industry. Like this, India has made an extraordinary mark in these seven spheres. We have to popularize it. It is very important today. These things should be recognized as a world heritage.

In life if you want satisfaction, then you need an ice factory in the brain, a sweet factory in the mouth and a compassion factory in the heart.

Whatever demands you have, surrender him/her to the Divine. Dukh (sadness) means tyaag ka bal (strength to surrender), and sukh (happiness) means seva ka bal (strength to serve).

In China, there was a popular person who had seven diseases. He started chanting OM every day for two hours and the diseases got cured. Sage Patanjali said this many years ago—If we chant OM every day, it reduces negative energy at home.

□

Understanding the Festival of Navratri

The festival of Navratri is celebrated with prayers and gaiety in the beginning of the Ashwin (autumn) and the beginning of Chaitra (spring). This period is a time for self-referral and getting back to the source. During this time of transformation, Nature sheds the old and gets rejuvenated; animals hibernate and life emerges back afresh in spring.

According to Vedic sciences, matter reverts to its original form to recreate itself again and again. The creation is cyclical, not linear; everything is recycled by Nature – a continuous process of rejuvenation. The human mind, however, lags behind in this routine cycle of creation. Navratri is a festival for one to take the mind back to its source.

The Mother Divine is recognized not just as the brilliance of intellect (buddhi), but also the confusion (bhranti); she is not just abundance (Lakshmi), she is also hunger (Shudha) and thirst (Trishna). Realizing this aspect of the Mother Divine in the entire creation, leads one to a deep state of Samadhi. This gives an answer to the age-old theological struggle of the Occident. Through wisdom, devotion and nishkama karma, one can attain advaita siddhi or perfection in the non-dual consciousness.

Kali is the most horrific manifestation of Nature. Nature symbolizes beauty, yet it has a horrific form. Acknowledging the duality brings a total acceptance in the mind and puts the mind at ease.

Though Navratri is celebrated as the victory of good over evil, the actual fight is not between good and evil. From the Vedantic point of view, the victory is of the absolute reality over the apparent duality. In the words of Ashtavakra, it is the poor wave which tries to keep its identity separate from the ocean, but to no avail.

The three primordial gunas are considered as the feminine force of our magnificent universe. By worshiping the Mother Divine during Navratri, we harmonize the three gunas and elevate sattva in the atmosphere.

The inward journey nullifies our negative karmas. Navratri is a celebration of the spirit or prana which alone can destroy mahishasura (inertia), shumbha-nishumbha (pride and shame) and madhu-kaitabh (extreme forms of craving and aversion). They are completely opposites, yet complementary. Inertia, deeply ingrained negativities and obsessions (raktabeejasura), unreasonable logics (chanda-munda) and blurred vision (dhoomralochan) can be overcome only by raising the level of prana and shakti, the life-force energy.

The seeker gets back to the true source through fasting, prayer, silence and meditation. Night is also called ratri because it brings rejuvenation. It gives relief at the three levels of our existence – physical, subtle and causal. While fasting detoxifies the body, silence purifies the speech and brings rest to the chattering mind, and meditation takes one deep into one's own being.

The nine days of Navratri are also an opportunity to rejoice in the three primordial qualities that make up the universe. Though our life is governed by the three gunas yet we seldom recognize and reflect on him/her. The first three days of Navratri are attributed to tamoguna, the next three days to rajoguna and the last three days to sattva guna. Our consciousness sails through the tamo and rajogunas and blossoms in the sattva guna of the last three days. Whenever sattva dominates in life, victory follows. The essence of this knowledge is honoured by celebrating the tenth day as Vijaydashmi.

Though the microcosm is very well within the macrocosm, its perceived separateness is the cause of conflict. For a gyani (wise), the entire creation becomes alive and he recognizes life in everything in the same way children see life in everything. The Mother Divine or the Pure Consciousness itself pervades all the forms and has all the names. Recognizing the one Divinity in every form and every name is the celebration of Navratri. Hence, special poojas honouring all the aspects of life and Nature are performed during the last three days. □

Understanding the Chanting of OM

OM is also called the sound of one-hand clapping. The sound which is generated in the universe, not out of friction! OM is an universal sound, so when people went deep in meditation, they heard it and they've been using it for millions of years. Recently, scientists who mapped the sound on the computer said that it has the same frequency as the earth's rotation around its own axis.

In the sound OM, our prana covers our whole body. OM has such a resonance with Nature – if you stand by the ocean and listen to the waves rolling, you will hear the sound OM. You go on top of a mountain and just listen to the wind blowing, you will hear the sound OM.

Maharishi Patanjali – the propounder of yoga said – to ward away all the obstacles in life, OM can be practised. It is one of the methods that he enunciates. Before meditation, when we sit and chant OM three times, and then use our mantra – whatever mantra we have been given, then meditation goes very deep.

In China, there is a very famous doctor who was suffering from seven major illnesses and he shared his experience. He said that it was his experience that he used to have 500 grams of medication every day to no avail. Then, he started chanting OM for one to two hours every day and in two years he was relieved of all diseases that were thought to be incurable. And his colleagues were surprised. Now this gentleman is calling it the music therapy and he is teaching this to people in China on national television.

When he shared his experience, I thought it is exactly what Maharishi Patanjali has said in the Yoga Sutras – Ek tattva abhyasa (practise the one tattva, one principle that is OM). It's called music therapy in China, chanting OM. Sound is nothing but energy. It's nothing but electricity. Our whole body is nothing but electricity.

And it can make a big impact on the cells of our body.

In guided meditation, you don't have to do anything. Meditation will be done for you. Just feel, 'Divinity is doing meditation for me, let me just relax.' Someone else is piloting the plane and you simply have to fasten the seatbelt, sit back and relax.

Don't use OM as a mantra for meditation because then there is an effort. It is good to enhance the prana as pranayama in the beginning or in the end. But don't sit and say, 'OM, OM, OM'. It may shoot up your energy too much and you may not know how to handle it. You may not get sleep.

In the beginning we chant OM three times, five times or seven times, and relax.

If you have fallen in love with somebody, there is no problem. You can definitely get married. Don't think there is no place for romance or romance is against spirituality. No, it is not. Promiscuity is against spirituality. Unethical exploitation of others is against spirituality. But if you are genuinely in love with a girl, and she is in love with you, it's okay. But if you are in love with somebody and she is in love with someone else, then you are in trouble and she is in trouble. The only person who would benefit in this case is the telephone company! And if you are in love, and your parents agree then it's great. But your romance should continue later too with the same person.

Last month a boy got married here and he said, 'I'm getting married to the same girl for the third time – first time was in America, then in Delhi and now, here.' This way, you can celebrate your romance every day. Spirituality is against any type of corruption. In the name of romance, if we are getting into lust and exploiting people, that is not right.

Romance is 'I am here for you. I want to share whatever I have with you.' It should come from a space of giving rather than grabbing. That romance is spiritual. In fact, in India, the concept of romance with the divine was brought out. Radha-Krishna are very well known throughout the country. □

Understanding the Mind-Time Connection

Time and mind are connected. You should know this. Time and mind are synonymous. It is said—'Desha, Kala, Manah'. Desha is space, Kala is time and, Manah – the mind. They are all tattvas, principles. And all these principles are connected. Desha and kala are connected. Space and time are connected. One day on this planet Earth is already many days on another…on the moon. On moon, it is different. So, if you are on Jupiter, one human year is only one month. In Jupiter, if you have to experience one year, that is 12 years of earthly time. Jupiter takes 12 years to go around the sun. Similarly, if you are on the planet Saturn, 30 years is one year!

Similarly, pitras, people who have died, our one year is one day for him/her. So our six months is only one night and six months is one day. So, for a soul which has departed our whole year is one day. There are different times and different space in different dimensions. So, time and space are connected. It's called the time-space curve. The same with the third dimension that is mind! The mindless, transcendental consciousness is called Mahakala, the Shiva, the fourth state of consciousness.

It's called Mahakala, means great time, and the no-mind. The no-mind is great time.

So, morning from 4.30 to 6.30, just before sunrise, before dawn, it's called the most creative time.

Brahma muhurta! And then, every two hours it's called a lagna; which means, one unit of time. And this unit of time corresponds to the state of mind. And again, this is connected with the moon's position, the sun's position. There are so many aspects! Ten different aspects influence the mind. So, not only the time or hour of the day affects the mind, but also the quality of the days affects the mind. Every

two and a half days the mind changes! The mood of the mind! So, if you are upset, it can continue for two and a half days at maximum; it doesn't have to be two and a half days. It rises to a peak and drops. But after two and a half days, you cannot have the same emotion with the same intensity. Impossible! It changes. Switches! It is a great, great science, how mind, mood and time are connected.

Jyotish shastra has a lot of insight into this. You know the astrologers, usually, all these weekly column astrologers say, 'Oh, good for relationships, good for making money, this and that!' They write those things. They generalize those things, 'If you are born on this time then this is good for you and you do this'. Of course, it's too generic and it's just a money-making thing that they do. But it is not a hoax; there is an iota of truth in it. The underlying base has truth. The principle that the mind and time are connected is correct.

Mind means moods, thoughts, opinions, ideas, all these things that we collect. And, no mind is meditation. Dawn and dusk are considered very good for meditation. So, whenever you meditate, or whenever the bad time is there, you meditate. When you meditate you go off the influence of the mind and go into the self. The self is Shiva tattva. Shiva tattva means, always benevolent, caring, loving, uplifting. That consciousness deep within you which is caring, loving, uplifting and benevolent, will nullify the negative influences of the mind and the time.

So, in India it is a very common belief, whenever there is bad time just say, 'OM Namah Shivaye,' and it's gone. All that bad time is gone. 'Manah', when read from the other side, it becomes Namah. Manah is when consciousness goes outside in the world, and Namah is when the consciousness goes inward. Shivaye, towards the Shiva principle, the fourth state of consciousness, the subtlest aspect of the existence, the Shiva tattva! So, Namah, when the mind goes towards the basic substratum of creation, then it can change all that into more benevolent experience.

It is not the promise which is important. What is important is:

what is best for everybody, for all human beings. Suppose you have promised your daughter to take her skiing but if the weather forecast says that there will be a snowstorm, what will you do? Will you take her out because you promised, or will you be intelligent and say, 'The promise will not bring happiness now, so I take back my promise and do not take you there now.'

When you have a sense of belongingness, shyness disappears.

The whole world is one family for me. You know, I feel absolutely at home wherever I am. I never have a feeling of being in a country or land that is not mine. I never felt strange anywhere. My concept is to see the whole world as one family; of course, family is a very important institution; it is the foundation of a society.

Jeeva is a part of Brahma. The balloon has air outside and inside it. Inside a vessel, there is space and outside there is space as well. The inside space is jeeva, the outside space is Brahma.

The jeeva is desire, aversion, craving. All this is the balloon. That is why the Lord is not somebody separate, but it is, 'What I am.' If the wave asks, 'Where is the ocean then what to say? The wave itself is the ocean. You have to realize this only. That is why it is said that while it takes a moment to break a flower stem, the Divine can be realized in a fraction of that moment.

If you think you shouldn't get disturbed, then you get more disturbed. The disturbance doesn't stay for all time. If there is some point in their comments, take it. Welcome the criticism. Is it for your improvement or is it the impression that you have created?

You doubt compliments. So doubt the criticism as well.

Right now are you happy or sad? Just be happy. So, the answer is within you.

Once, a woman went to a saint and asked, 'Why is the world so sad?'

If you can't leave the world when there is unhappiness, how will you leave a world full of happiness?

You will be in a great loss if you can't let go of the world. Just turn inwards to the source, there is no sadness. Once you have learnt how to go inwards, the world doesn't seem sad.

Just look at the world, where is the sadness? Birds are chirping; the river is flowing. Where is the sadness? I only see beauty in the world. Just look at all the faces; they are so happy!

In life, there's 20 per cent sadness and 80 per cent happiness. But our mind makes the 20 per cent into 2000 per cent.

One of the main reasons for poverty is alcoholism.

Many villagers spend 60 per cent of their earnings in the toddy shop. If you think they are poor, then from where have they got toddy? Villages have risen above the poverty line just by closing the toddy shops. The poorest of the poor can earn and do not stay hungry, wherever alcohol has stopped. Youngsters in rural areas are now dealing with this problem.

People of all castes should celebrate together. Everyone should come together for one meal in a week. When people in the village come together, then the feeling of Dalit and non-Dalits will be removed. In every village, ask those who can contribute for those who don't have enough. Such development cannot be done by the government alone. NGOs have to initiate this change.

Do you feel belongingness? That is spirituality.

When this belongingness expands to include everyone, then spirituality has grown.

Suppose you sit for four-five hours. Do you get a pain in your legs? How do you know? Our doubt is always about something positive. Someone asks, 'Are you happy?' And we say, 'Well…I am not sure.'

You never doubt your depression.

In order to discuss about true contentment, we need to be in a cordial and informal atmosphere. Do you all agree with this? It is important that we feel at home. A formal atmosphere is not congenial to discuss something that is so close to your heart. Why not we take a couple of minutes to greet people around us? You know, why do we feel very dry in life? Because we live in a very formal world. Our greetings are so formal, our sorry is formal. So, we live in a world which is just words without feelings and presence behind it. Suppose you go as a guest to somebody's house and he is just formally greeting you. Do you feel satisfied? You know, if you go into the huts of people in Indian villages. There is greeting that comes from the innocence of their hearts. It touches your heart. Otherwise, most of the pleasantries we exchange are like the words of airhostesses saying, 'Have a nice day.' They don't mean it. Today, we have forgotten to be authentic. Why have we built walls between us? Sometimes I wonder people are so formal even with their own children. We have built solid boundaries around us, isn't it so? We speak and convey more through our presence than through our words. I often say that a dog is a better communicator than human beings. It cannot speak your language but it conveys the sense of belongingness through its actions and behaviour. It breaks all the barriers to express its love. It does not mind jumping on you even if you are wearing new dress. It invades your boundaries and expresses itself. True contentment can come when we are in touch with our core being, our selves. And what helps in that to happen is releasing the stress.

Many times, those who appear to be enemies are not actually enemies. I would give you an example of what we did in Iraq. We gave some meditation and Sudarshan Kriya to the troubled youth there. There was such a huge transformation in him/her. The youth minister sent 50 youth leaders to the 'Art of Living' international centre in Bangalore to be trained as ambassadors of peace. It was challenging to begin with, but there was amazing transformation in

him/her in a period of one month. The same boys went back and started to teach thousands of people how to be calm. You know, we are not taught how to manage negative emotions neither at home nor at school. You get angry, upset, greedy or depressed, but we are not taught how to manage our mind.

I am not saying that we have solutions to resolve all the conflicts in the worlds tomorrow itself. It is not practical. But what has given us hope is, after experiencing meditation, there is enormous change in the same people who appear to be aggressive or enemies.

In 2001, there was a difficult situation in Kashmir. But things have changed now. We can make effort drop by drop. In Jahanabad also, our efforts have given good results. All this has given me enthusiasm to go in all conflict zones and do more work. Though, it is a big challenge.

When some people think that only they will go to heaven and others to hell, they create hell for others. We need to educate him/her with a broader mindset. So, every child should know little bit about all the world's wisdom. We have globalized things like potato chips but we haven't globalized wisdom, and education on peace and non-violence. When people are stressed, they either become violent and aggressive or suicidal tendencies arise in him/her. The solution for depression, suicidal tendencies, social and domestic violence is to teach him/her how to calm their minds. It is very important to teach him/her how they can get rid of negative emotions, stress, and all those unwanted emotions. How can we heal him/her? That healing touch is essential.

A woman has a great role to play. Women can influence many men around him/her – father, brother, children, spouse. They have more power and more influence. In Indian mythology, all the powerful portfolios like defence ministry, finance and education are with women. What else do you want? In India we believe man and woman are equal partners. There is a concept of Ardhnareeshvar – God is neither male nor female. Divine is half male and half female. Everyone is like that. Nobody is full male or full female. There are genes of both mother and father within each one of us. So, we must respect women.

Women should take more lead in the society. And I think that women can be better peace makers, and then less conflict, greed and corruption will be there in the world. Corruption can only happen outside the boundary of belongingness. Heart can never be corrupt. It is the mind which goes corrupt. Heart always longs for old and mind for new, isn't it so? You want more and more in mind but the heart says, 'I am happy.' Heart wants to give and the mind wants to take. Women are more with their hearts. They should keep that quality while developing leadership and taking more social responsibility.

In the morning, the mind is in a state of knowledge, alertness and wakefulness. It is action-oriented in the afternoon and in the evening, the mind is in a state of relaxation. One who wants to be unhappy can be unhappy the whole time, and one who wants to be happy can be happy throughout the day. A fool will be unhappy all the time and the intelligent one will be happy in spite of changing moods.

We are all one. I am you and you are me.

See, the mind is like space. The self is like space inside and outside the body. The thoughts come and go, emotions come and go, but when you go inside there is only empty space. And our true nature is that. When we identify ourselves too much with thoughts, with feelings and emotions, that is when we feel we are stuck, we are small. But, the 'Real, Magnanimous You' are that space inside where you feel totally at peace. Those moments when you are totally in peace or fully in love, you feel an expansion, right? You feel boundless, you feel limitless, and that is our true nature. That is what the beauty is. We are all one in that, there is no two!

Our mind feels and perceives differently in the morning than it does in the evening.

The placement of planets also affects the mind. Sometimes faith arises in the mind, sometimes hatred envelopes the mind. It is natural for the different waves of emotions to rise in the mind.

I am separate from all this, I am atma. Contemplating on this is the sign of intelligence.

It is often believed that glory and dispassion are contradictory and cannot co-exist. Glory and luxury without dispassion is a nauseating pomp and show. Such glory does not bring fulfilment for anyone… it is shallow. Alternately, the dispassion that is afraid of glory is weak. True dispassion is oblivious to glory.

The glory that comes with dispassion is something that is true, that is permanent and authentic. When someone runs after glory, he/she is shallow. Like movie stars, politicians and religious leaders who try to hold onto their status, to their glory, they are certain to lose. If you run after glory all you get is misery. When you are dispassionate, glory comes to you.

If you are afraid of glory, that means you are not well-founded in dispassion. In India, the Sadhus run away from glory. They think they will lose their dispassion and get trapped in the web of the world, the circus. The dispassion is so blissful that they get attached to the dispassion. (laughter)

They are afraid of losing the dispassion, the centredness and bliss that comes along with it. This is weak dispassion. Dispassion is a state of being and glory is the happening around it. True dispassion can never be lost or overshadowed by glory.

True dispassion is glorious!
Real glory is true dispassion!

Do not put off the fire of longing for the Divine or satsang with dispassion.

There is a little fire in you that propels you towards knowledge, sadhana, devotion and service. Sometimes you use knowledge to put off that fire. The so-called dispassionate people are often morose and unenthusiastic. Many a time you hear people saying, 'Oh, never mind; God is everywhere; Guruji is in my heart; you can do satsang

anywhere. My seva is my sadhana, so no need to meditate; anyway, I am doing sadhana twenty-four hours. When God wills, He will call me to satsang and advanced courses again!'

Such excuses should not be justified as dispassion.

When you want to do some service, the mind goes, 'Oh, it's all Maya, anyway everything is an illusion. It's all just happening. Things will happen when the time comes!'

In this way knowledge gets misused and is quoted out of context to suit one's convenience or laziness. In the name of dispassion do not lose that spark of enthusiasm and interest. Using knowledge like this you miss out a lot.

Keep the fire of longing for the Divine and service to the society alive. Dispassion here would be detrimental.

There is a strange relationship between love and truth. If there is a competition between love and truth, it is love that will win. It is the fear of losing love that makes someone tell lies to the most loved ones. He/she is afraid of losing him/her love if he/she tells the truth. So, which is powerful? Love is powerful. And it should be that way. What is love? If you have not known, there is no way you will know. Even a single creature on this planet cannot say that it doesn't know love, because that is our second experience. Our first experience was pain.

Harmony in sound is music; harmony in movement is dance; harmony in mind is meditation; harmony in life is celebration.

Love is the mother of all negative emotions. All those who lose their temper are perfectionists. They want everything perfect, they simply love perfection. They have high pitta (a characteristic of the body as per the ancient science of Ayurveda). They seek perfection in everything. Jealousy is because of love. You love somebody so jealousy arises. Greed is when you love objects more than people.

Arrogance is when you love yourself too much. Arrogance is to love oneself in a distorted manner. Not even a single object on this planet wants not to be loved or be away from love. Yet we don't want any of the pain or suffering that comes along with love. How can one achieve this? Only through cleansing and uplifting our spirit which is possible through spirituality. We are made up of both matter and spirit. Our body needs vitamins. If any nutrient is missing then we have a deficiency. Similarly, we are made up of spirit. Spirit is beauty, truth, joy, happiness, love and peace. For me, spirituality is that which enhances all these qualities and removes the boundaries. We can bring up our children and youth in this spiritual way. Nowadays violence in college campuses is common. This is unfortunate. If there is violence then there is something fundamentally wrong. There was so much pride attached to non-violence and equanimity when I was growing up. Schools and colleges will have to bring about peace, happiness, celebration and joy. But if we are miserable, we cannot bring happiness to anybody. First, we need to attend to our misery. It's a catch 22. If you are not happy, you can't do anything to make others happy. So how can you be happy? Unless you think from a broader perspective, you cannot be happy.

There is a technique to get depressed. If you just sit and think about yourself all the time, 'What about me, what about me?' you will get depressed. We need to engage ourselves in some service activities and spiritual practices that eliminate negative vibes and make our presence lighter, happier, more content and more intuitive. Intuition is essential. If you are a businessman, you need intuition to know which stocks to invest in. If you are a poet or a literary person, you need intuition. If you are a doctor, you need intuition. Doctors don't base the prescription just on observation. There is something else that also contributes to the prescription. All doctors here will agree with me. Intuition can come when we look deep inside. Without intuition and a spiritual connection, it is like using a cell phone without a sim card in it. We pray, but we are not connected at all. Then we

wonder why our prayers are not answered. Because there is no spirituality and values inside, and hence no connectivity is there. This is how many people become atheists. An incident happens in their life, their prayers didn't work, and they get illusioned.

Each one of us has enormous potential. Your thoughts are very powerful; you can create what you want. It's not like you can go to the moon tomorrow, but for that to happen the vision has to come first. The intuitive power has to come. First, believe that it is possible for you to live in a state of unconditional love, peace and tranquility. As a child, you have lived in this state. As children, we all have done it. We were bubbling with enthusiasm.

I am with you. You are not alone. If anyone any time feels lonely, depressed, unhappy or sad, just remember that you are not alone. You are not alone at all.

Spirituality will become more fashionable in the coming years; people will become more spiritual. Everyone will understand more about the consciousness. Right here, there are so many layers of the universe and existence. More and more of it will come to light. People will understand; science will also discover.

Doubt is always about something that is positive. You know, if someone tells you that he/she loves you, you say, 'Really? Isn't it so?' But you take it for granted when someone expresses his/her hatred towards you. If someone asks you, 'Are you happy?' you say, 'Well, I am not sure.' We doubt all that is positive. We doubt in love. We doubt in the goodness of people. We doubt honesty. We never doubt dishonesty. Isn't it so? We doubt our capabilities. We never doubt our weaknesses. You never doubt your depression, but you always doubt your happiness. So, a doubt is always about something that is positive.

Sitting close by and listening is Upanishad. The Upanishad is a collection of discourses of high knowledge; how it was transmitted from a Master to students. It is very interesting.

In one of the Upanishads, it is beautifully said–

Once a boy goes to his father who is also his Guru and asks him what God is. Father replied, 'Food is God', for everything grows from food, everything is sustained by food and in the lack of it, everything dissolves and everything again becomes food. So, the boy went and thought about it for several months, understood all about food and came back to his father, and again asked, 'What is God?'

The father, also his Guru, said, 'Prana is God.' The boy went, thought and understood all about prana, how it is going in and out of the body, how many types of prana are there and read all experiments about prana.

He again came back to his father and asked, 'What is God?' The father looked at his child's face, so glowing and so vibrant. He said, 'OK, the mind is Brahman, 'mind is God.'

Like that, the boy went and thought till he found the Ultimate Bliss. Neither, does the student complain to the teacher that he was told, 'Food is God, but it is not the ultimate, you told me the wrong thing.' He simply came and again asked the question. So, this is the ancient way of teaching step by step – food, then prana, then the mind, then the inner spirit, then the Universal Spirit, bliss.

Bliss is Divinity, space. You are like space. Then he said, 'There is no difference between you, me and the infinite self. We all are one. The Self, The Guru and the Universal Energy are not different. All are made up of one substance. Today if you talk to scientists who study string theory, who study quantum physics they will say the same thing that is said in the Upanishads.

In the Upanishads, it was said thousands of years ago, 'God is not a person, sitting somewhere up in heaven but God is present everywhere. He is omnipresent and omnipotent, the energy of which you are also made up, everything is made up'.

There is no control over the fruit of action. If the attention is

only on the end result, then you can't perform. Let us take a runner – if he starts looking behind at who is running, and not looking at the path he needs to run on, then ultimately he will lose, no matter how good the runner may be. You have to follow your own track, to complete the run whether you lose or win. Lord Krishna is utterly practical in his advice. Lord Krishna tells Arjuna – This is complex, but these are the ways to do it.

Objects need me but I don't need objects. After the first two becomes strong, then three. The car needs me but I don't need it. This world needs me but I don't need the world. You don't have to reject externally but know in your mind. Even your body is an object. This is subtle. But when this knowledge dawns, there can never be poverty. We keep thinking, 'We need this and that.' But when we have the dharana that 'the Divine cares for me and I don't need anything', then your needs are taken care of anyway.

Waves come and go. In the world, all are happy at all times – this is not possible. The importance of food is when there is hunger. If there is no hunger in the world, what to do with food?

Conflict is always emotional. Resolution is intellectual. Emotional conflict can't be dealt with emotions. Similarly, an intellectual argument cannot be dealt with the intellect. The emotional side of it has to be considered. If you observe carefully, there is a stream of emotions behind an intellectual argument. Life is a fine balance between the emotions and the intellect. When to use what, is the real wisdom. And how do you gain that wisdom? The answer is meditation, meditation and meditation.

Love is present everywhere. It is the intelligent who keep the love from being distorted. Love when distorted becomes greed, jealousy, fear and hatred.

When a person is involved – it gives rise to moha – obsession.

Anger comes out of love for perfection.

Behind every emotion, positive and negative, there is love. There is no existence without love. We want love, pure love without misery, which brings joy and peace. Pure love turns into bliss. The spiritual path keeps the love away from greed and puts you on the other side – bliss and joy.

Thoughts are energy, have power. When you are confused, your words don't have an impact. The clearer you are in your mind, the more power your words get. If you are in confusion, the power of words is very feeble. Pranayama, meditation makes the mind clear. So the thoughts that come out of it are straight and clear. One who is content, their words have power.

In India, we have a custom of going to our elders for blessings. They are supposed to have a serene state of mind. From that space, when you give a blessing, it is more effective. For wedding cards, blessings are taken from the eldest member of the family. The same tradition exists in North America, Australia and New Zealand among the native people. All over the world, native traditions have the custom of respecting elders. Without this, people above 50 are getting depressed. That has to shift.

Parents should also become more happy and vibrant.

Happier as you grow older! The older you are, the bigger your smile – satisfied, fulfilled. You have led a good life. Now you only have to bless people of the coming generations. That is maturity. That is satisfaction. This comes when you become detached from day-to-day things. Wash your hands off anything that makes you unhappy. Take on your responsibility. Act for it but don't worry for it. People who act don't worry and those who worry don't act. This shift has to come. Otherwise, you keep complaining, so and so doesn't listen, the daughter-in-law doesn't listen.

You should not go to your grave with complaints. Do only what

you can. Stretch yourself little by little. Like this, we need to re-orient ourselves. We are either complacent or complaining. Either is no good. Then you remain without doing any action. On the other hand, till the last breath, if you find fault with others, that is also no good.

When a robber enters your door, you start shaking, shivering, questioning; it's of no use. Why did the robber rob you is a useless question. It's his job! Accept he is a robber. Somebody cheats you. When you are caught up in asking why he cheated. You become upset, and you can't take action. When you accept the robber, then you call the police, etc. You can take action. Parents get upset over the child not studying. Accept. Then you can act better. If you don't accept, emotions rise, intellect is clouded and actions become regrettable.

Relief from trauma comes only through meditation. Counselling is only at the surface. The source of joy is deep within. Events are impermanent. You will not allow any event to stick on to the mind mirror. You are unfazed by events. Keeping the mind like a clean mirror – that is what yoga is all about. People not on the spiritual path never feel fulfilled.

People say a knowledgeable person is one who kills one's feelings, No, it's not like that. Sadbhav, saintly feelings continue to exist. Lord Krishna also said in the Bhagwad Gita, 'One who is not tied to me – the Consciousness, Higher Self – neither has intellect nor feelings. 'Without feelings and intellect, there is no question of peace or happiness.'

□

Understanding Dharma and Sangha

Dharma and sanga. Our innermost nature is what dharma is. Yes, our innermost nature is dharma and sangha is our association, our environment.

So events and attitudes are influenced by only two things.

The first is by your own true nature and another by your environment, the people whom you are with, you know. In a group, if someone says, 'Come, let's go and have a drink,' we will say, 'Ok; let's all go.' We will go. In a group, if someone starts talking negatively, slowly another person will join a little later, then the third and the fourth. Soon you'll find that everybody starts talking negatively – this is the influence of the group. A child is influenced up to 25 per cent by the environment, by the friends in the environment and the school he/she grows up in. Another 25 per cent is from the parents' genes and tendencies. The next 25 per cent is his/her own originality, his/her karmas, his/her samskaras, the impression that he/she comes into this world with. The remaining 25 per cent is through his/her own self-effort and his/her understanding. So parents have got only one-fourth influence on their children. Only one-fourth. Similarly, our sangha which means our association has an influence on us. Usually, what we call sangha is a group of people who are on the spiritual path. People on the spiritual path can help you with that much-needed energy, biodiversity energy for you to move on that path. That is why when you sit and meditate in a group, it is better than when you are alone. How many of you feel that way? In a group, you feel like doing yoga, pranayama, even service activity. When you are alone, you get tired. You don't feel like doing it. But a few of you join together and you do a lot of work.

If you have to wash the dishes alone, you will feel so bored.

But if 7, 8 or 9 of us are washing the dishes, time just flies like that. You don't feel tired. I have told you don't feel exhausted, isn't it? How many of you have this experience? At home, if someone is asked to wash that many dishes, you would crib. And here you do it with the smile, you do it happily, joyfully. So sangha can, or the group sangha can help you move up in life. It puts you in touch with dharma; and sangha only happens with the enlightened. That's why Lord Buddha said – Buddham, sangham and dharmam. Three things – the enlightened one, the company of people and your true nature – all these things are important and they all are one and the same.

You can meditate any time when your tummy is not full. When you have eaten, you are full. When you sit for meditation at that time, that is not good. Either you will not have meditation, you'll fall asleep or you'll have indigestion. There will be some difficulty in metabolism.

Politicians have lost the sense of belongingness with people. Politics has become another industry. It has ceased to be a place for responsibility and caring and protection of people's welfare. Rather, it has turned out to be self-aggrandizement, an industry of power and position and money. This has to change. You know, politicians will have to realize that they are the servants of people. They have responsibilities. There are some very good politicians. Not that we should put him/her all in the same basket. But those corrupt politicians are the ones we really need to address. That can happen only through education and rising awareness of human values among him/her. I am very much concerned, especially about Africa, where people have very little to eat. The country is really going down and the politicians of Africa have hoarded billions – $280 billion – in a bank in England. When I was speaking to the politicians at the European parliament, they told me, 'Guruji, we have a good news. We have sent $79 million back to Africa to the people there because it's the people's money. But it's not sufficient. It's only a small portion of what the presidents and the prime ministers of the continent of Africa are holding there. Similarly, Indian politicians are holding huge amounts in Swiss banks. But it's all been hushed up. There needs to be a wave of spiritual awakening, moral and spiritual awakening in the whole world, especially in this field. Only then can this be corrected.

So, it's a big task. Everybody has to work for it. We need politicians like Gandhi and Martin Luther King who were spiritual and who cared for people to uphold ideals in society.

There is only one air, one sun, one earth and one moon. Similarly, there is only one consciousness. In the inside of us, the consciousness which is wisdom, which is light is gurutattva. Tattva means principle. To begin with, the five tattvas are Earth, Water, Air, Ether and Fire. These are five tattvas and then there is the mind, intellect and ego. Then there is the maha tattva which is beyond the ego. The one who has gone beyond the ego is called Mahatma. Finer than the maha tattva is the gurutattva. The gurutattva is that principle of discrimination, of knowledge and when it dawns inside you, that is gurutattva. In knowledge then, you have no dearth for anything. Life's mission is complete. Gurutattva always brings joy, freedom from misery and uplift of the consciousness.

Judgment is a set of concepts which appears to be obsolete. An opinion or a concept which becomes obsolete, you call it judgment. Not the judgment that the judge gives in the court, but the one you come up with. You have an opinion of a person, or a concept, or a situation, when that breaks then you look back and you say, 'Oh, I have a judgment of it.' If it doesn't break, that's, when you say, 'Oh, I know it is knowledge, oh you know I know that's how it is.' You call it judgment when it is obsolete; that means it has broken or proved to be false. Right?

Judgment is the opposite of intuition, intuition is the right opinion. Judgment is the wrong opinion.

The sound of 'Om namah shivaya' includes all the five elements – Earth, Water, Fire, Air and Ether. Hinduism is not a religion as such. People have been chanting this for thousands of years. Mantras are those sounds which you hear from deep within during meditation and the aim is to bring one back to the source. During later days, people started putting faces and drawings to these mantras. Mantras have got certain vibrations/energy. They are universal.

Even in churches in Latin America 'Marnah nath' is used. Its translation in Latin and Sanskrit is so close. For 'Lord', the word in Latin is nath and also in Sanskrit, the word nath is used to mean 'Lord'. So the word marnah nath meaning 'My Lord' which is used in Christianity is actually a Sanskrit word.

Misery simply means you are stuck to the outside. Joy means you are in your element which is inside. If you depend on others for your comfort, you lose your joy. First, have this faith that Nature will provide whatever I need, or I deserve. It will never happen that Nature doesn't provide you with what you need. Secondly, I want nothing from anybody. And the third whatever I have, it is only for others and I will serve others as much as I can. Finish! Where is the misery then?

Saying 'I love you' every day and every time, it eventually turns into, 'I can't stand you!' Too much expression spoils things. If you don't express at all, that is also not good. There needs to be moderation. Just like a seed – it does not germinate if you scatter it on the surface nor if you bury it too deep. It needs to be sown at just the right depth. In the same way, moderation is necessary.

Have you seen lemon juice under the microscope? It looks like the rays of the sun. When you see vitamin C under the microscope, it looks like a sunflower. Some substances like salt, lemon, chillies etc. have the potential to remove negativity. In the West, bathing in

the ocean for rejuvenation and improving health is popular. The burdens, the worries in the mind, harmful influences are reduced in this way. Faith also works here. Even when you take regular medicines, if you don't have faith in the doctor or the medication, it may not help you at all.

When you try to keep hold of your mind, it runs here and there. When you become aware of the wandering mind then you realize you are bigger than the mind. When you find you are not this mind, not this body, not anything else, whatever remains is the Self. Knowing your Self, recognize the Supreme Self. Then you find you are everything. You are the mind, the thoughts, you are the whole world. But that happens at the second level. When you know your Self, you know the Divine. Sarvam Kalvidam Brahma – Everything is One Divinity. Knowing this, become established in this knowledge.

Only a rich person can make others also rich. Only a liberated one can bring freedom to others. Only a devotee can evoke devotion in others. A person in love with the Divine makes others also like that. Whatever is there within you, that is, what others receive and, that is, what you perceive in others.

The more sattva/purity rises in your life, the more easily your tasks get accomplished. The amount of sattva/ purity in us decides the productivity of our input. If you put in a lot of effort and the result turns out to be less or below your expectations, it means that there is a lack of sattva/ purity in life. When we meditate then our work happens easily. People are unaware of this secret. It is very important to meditate whenever we get time so that you may accomplish your tasks more efficiently and with ease.

There are four levels of speech – para, pashyanti, madhyama, vaikari.

The language we speak is vaikari. It is the most manifest form

of speech. Chatvari vak parimita padani – there are four levels of speech and the intelligence knows all forms. Human beings speak only the fourth level. Subtler than vaikari, is madhyama. Even before you say it, the thought form is cognized. When you catch it at that level, it is madhyama. Pashyanti is cognitive. There is no need for spoken words. Para is the untold, un-manifest knowledge that is beyond.

□

Understanding the Creation of the Universe

The whole universe is spherical. It was never born nor shall it ever die. It is anadi – beginningless; and anantha – endless. Then what is the job of Brahma, the creator? They say there are many, many Brahma, Vishnu and Shiva in every yuga (age). In time and space, this keeps happening. So what is the source of this creation? Parame vyoman – beyond the akasha (space). Knowledge lies beyond the akasha. Knowledge lies beyond the five elements.

Richo akashare parame vyoman.

The Vedas which were cognized are not vaikari. This cognition is beyond space. All the Divine impulses are established in that field which is all permeating.

What is akasha? Akasha is described as vyoma, vyapti – it means all-permeating, all-pervading. What is it that is beyond akasha? It is unimaginable to think of something that is beyond space. Only a scientist can understand this. Everything is contained in akasha, all the four elements are in akasha. The most gross is Earth, then Water, Fire, Air and Space. Air is finer, subtler than Fire. Space is the subtlest. Then it is Air, Fire, Water and Earth. What is it that is beyond even akasha? That is the mind, intellect, ego and the Mahatattva. This is tattva gyan – knowing the principle of the universe. Unless you know the principle of the universe, you cannot know the Self. When you go beyond the akasha, it is an experiential field. The whole realm begins beyond the akasha.

The ancient seers have spoken about the Dravya guna sambandha, or relationship between the substance and its quality. There is a very interesting debate if we can separate the quality from the substance.

The whole philosophy is very interesting and the conclusion was that you cannot separate the quality from the substance. Can the sweetness in sugar be separated from sugar? Will it remain sugar still? Can heat and light be separated from fire? Will it still be fire after that?

What brings the quality into the substance? What comes first – the quality or the substance? There are many questions like this. The subtler you go is the parame vyoman. Yasmin devaadhi vishwe nishedu – all the devis and devtas reside there, in that space. Yattanaveda yati vaanaveda – what is the use of knowing the Vedic hymns and mantras without knowing the parame vyoman, without understanding the principles of the universe?

Swarupa is the quality of that space. It cannot be fully translated in English. Swarupa is that consciousness. From the Swarupa happens the Sputa or explosion from which svarita, creation flows and sakaara – manifests with name and form. All the millions of beings in the creation were formed from the swarupa.

Parmatma is the sun, devta is its ray. Without the sun, there is no ray and without the ray, there is no sun. A ray has all seven colours; these are different devtas. God is the combination of all the seven colours. God is certainly not made of one colour. When all colours combine, white is obtained and that is Parmatma. You can understand this like different organs – eyes, ears, nose, all combine to form you. The totality of the whole creation, with all the energies is given a name and it is called Parmatma, Parampita (Supreme Father). In ancient terminology, God is called Parmatma, Parampita.

Mantras are those sounds which you hear from deep within during meditation and the aim is to bring one back to the source.

What is a sign of the dawning of wisdom? Prasanna chitta (pleasant state of mind) is a sign. Friendliness, foresight, intuition, a mind in the present moment – these are the signs of wisdom.

Once you are able to see the light, you see the entire past as a dream; then move on. Wake up and see the present, you will find happiness is there, unconditional happiness. Then you are happy and not dependant on others for your happiness. Happiness depends only on your mind. When the mind is free of past impressions and future cravings, happiness is there.

Prayer is asking, meditation is listening. In prayer, you ask, 'Give me this, give me that', giving instructions, demanding. In meditation, you say, 'I am here to listen, what is it that you want to tell? Tell me, whenever you are free, I am here. The culmination of prayer is meditation. Prayer goes to the peak and that is meditation.

Against such knowledge, you will not be able to give me anything. If you really want to give me anything, give me your worries, your pain, leave it for me here as your dakshina. And the other thing that you can do is seva. Spread smiles to everyone you come across. But even that won't make 1/10th of what I have given you. And surrender every good thing that you do, know that you are offering guru dakshina. □

Understanding the Science behind Spirituality

You know, our body is constantly emitting energy, vibrations. You are emitting energy all the time. And when you know your vibrations is what makes things happen in the world, you will know that you are in control. So when you are thinking that things are going to be negative then that is what seed you are putting in the universe, and that is going to happen. So with your positive thinking, positive ideas, positive sankalpa… It is said, let positive vibrations come out of you.

Negative thoughts arise in you, yet you say, everything is positive. And how does that happen? Not by just thinking, but by relaxing. Cutting a thought with another thought is only superficial but cutting a thought by silence, by letting go, by devotion, by faith, by surrendering to God, it is deeper.

Maharishi Patanjali says that the poise of mind happens when you offer all that you can't handle yourself to God, to the Universal Spirit.

The Universal Spirit is all around you, all the time. It doesn't have a form, a name, but it is around you all the time and you surrender your desires to that Universal Spirit. Be sure and know that your problem is going to be solved. That is siddhi, perfection. You notice in your own life, be centred, relax and let go and you will see things are happening effortlessly; it has to happen that way and if you don't find that way, then there is some screw in the mind that is loose, that needs to be fixed.

People ask for blessings and I give blessings in abundance, blank cheques of blessings, but you should know how to fill it, encash it and the way to encash it is, 'It is going to be done', 'My needs will

be taken care of', 'Best will be done; without a question. Sometimes we don't know what we desire, or we desire for something that we don't deserve, or we desire for something much less than what we deserve. Ask and it will be given. When we deserve more and desire for less, ask skilfully. So, what is the way? Ask skilfully, and how: 'I want this or anything better than this.' And have that positive frame of mind because it's all neurons. One of the scientists says that our brain has different types of neurons, and there are certain neurons which create barriers.

When a person in front of you touches someone else, the brain says, 'You are being touched' but there are certain neurons in hand which sends a signal to the brain that says, 'It is not you being touched.' If your hand is given anaesthesia and then if someone touches someone else, you will also feel the touch. And he (the scientist) says, we all are nothing but neurons, we all are connected, everybody is connected. The subtler we go, we find there are only vibrations, and there are no neutrons, protons, electrons but all that exists is – vibrations. And then he says numbers are very important.

In Rudrapooja, we say 'ekachame, trisraschame…', yesterday only we understood why we said that. We chant odd numbers first and then even numbers in the Rudrapooja. He said if numbers won't be there, the whole universe will collapse. Everything exists on numbers, on figures and if one number goes missing, the whole universe will collapse. It's like on a cell phone you want to make a call and if you dial one wrong digit the call never goes to the right person. One can't argue saying, 'if one digit is wrongly dialed? And if everything is right then life gets connected; so numbers are so important. And it is all just vibration.

One of the greatest physicists who were in the team of creating the first nuclear bomb dropped on Hiroshima and Nagasaki says, 'I studied matter for 35 years to find out it doesn't exist. What exists is just vibration.' Everyone of us is emitting and absorbing vibrations. And chanting, singing creates such a positive vibration, you become a source of energy.

What is the difference between a bulb, which is lit and a bulb which is not? One is emitting energy and in the other, no energy

movement is there. And all singing, chanting and meditating is like lighting the bulb. Have you noticed the difference between those who are doing all this with faith and someone who has never done this? It reflects on their faces. If you haven't started noticing, you should better start noticing.

What happens when you are worrying all the time? Suddenly you find the brain, the upper part has become like a stone, the heart has become like a stone. Similarly, what happens when you hear a negative comment about yourself from somebody? The whole body has become heavy. You can't avoid people saying negative things about you. How many have this question? And how many have this experience? When someone says something negative about you or when a close friend of you is feeling very low, suddenly, you also start feeling the same, your whole energy goes down. That is why satsang is that important, this knowledge is that important.

When you focus on someone who is depressed, you also feel the same and when you participate in a satsang your whole focus is shifted to knowledge. That's why the Guru is important because when you think of the Guru, when you shift your focus to the Guru in a few moments, your energy gets restored, you get back to your normal self. How many of you have experienced this?

There is an old proverb 'Guru bina gati nahin', which means there is no progress without the Guru; because there are so many people around you and you are being tossed and turned by everybody's moods, emotions and blames, and you are stuck, you can't notice that. But when a Guru is there nothing of this will matter to you and even if it does it is only for a few minutes or hours and then you are able to push through it, move through it. Like you have a rain coat and if it is raining you can always protect yourself from rain. In this context ancient people in India, Korea, Japan, even in China, had said that spiritual teacher, master or a person who is on the path is so important, so that you may not have to keep feeling these negative vibrations, heaviness for days together.

Secondly, if you find nobody is available, no commune is available then what do you do? Chant, do pranayama, Nature walk, Vedanta or this science that everything is just vibrations.

Numbers are very important, so we chant 'Om Namah Shivaya' 108 times. In Islam also, they put a number 786, right? In Rudra Abhishek we chant an odd and even sequence of numbers. That changes the vibrations. Even pundits don't have the answers of chanting numbers in Rudra Abhishek. We have to listen to the scientists to understand. They say this whole space is curved. Space is also like water, like you put a ball in water, it curls. Water is a medium, like that space is also a medium and this was also said thousands of years ago in the Vedas. That is why, it is the fifth element. Space is where vibration travels, it is a medium like water, air, fire and earth. And the same thing scientists are saying today. It is amazing to see how people 10,000 years ago knew that space has a curvature, it is a medium and there are not 1 but 10 dimensions, which is the spirit. These facts open your mind to a higher reality.

The solar plexus is called the second brain or mid brain. For a yogi, the solar plexus is larger in size. Scientists have also said this. It is small in a person who doesn't do yoga and meditation. A yogi who does meditation and yoga has a larger solar plexus. When solar plexus is larger, creativity dominates and generosity rises. When it is smaller, jealousy arises!

When your heart opens up, tears come; it's natural. Let it be. It is said in scriptures that the tears of love are so precious that even angels run to collect it. Even in heaven, there are no tears of love. The most wonderful thing on the planet, on the earth is to have the tears of love, tears of gratitude. That indicates that our life is glorious. That makes our life rich and fulfilled. Fulfilment in life is when you have the tears of gratitude and that comes by luck. You can't manufacture the tears of gratitude; you can't put glycerine and have the tears of gratitude coming in. When you realize what all you have received in life, your heart opens up.

There is only One doer. It is not your doing, but your Being.

You don't become a saint with what you have done, but with who you are. How much compassion, service, love one has in one's heart. The job gets done with the collective effort of so many people. But if we want our inner being to shine then your own intention is enough.

Do not leave your passion for God. Whatever experience we are getting is due to His Grace, not through our efforts. If you are able to love everybody, it is a Blessing! We have to be grateful...the more grateful we are, the more we get. What do you say?

I unequivocally condemn casteism. There is no caste for the spirit. When we want to see a good doctor, we don't ask his caste. When we want to see a good lawyer, we don't ask his caste. It is of use only in politics! I don't know politics. I speak from my heart to your heart. I love to be with the people of God.

When nothing is of help, prayer helps! A genuine 'Help me God!'

Any challenge is a chance to reaffirm our commitment!

The best pilgrimage is the Inward Journey! A pilgrimage is an opportunity for people to come together and pray together. As you know, praying together generates more energy, you know, a synergy. But don't think God is only in pilgrim centres! God is omnipresent and omniscient. Ancient Rishis meditated in some places and put all that energy in some idol there. Scriptures talk about God as having no name and no form. There is freedom to worship God in any form or any name. Wisdom from anywhere was acknowledged.

We have to educate the society about the ONE divinity. When that shift happens, we can relate to anybody, whatever be our ideology.

Fear will be eliminated. Inside every culprit, there is a victim crying for help... what is troubling him?... He could have been a victim of ignorance or brainwashing or violence...

The contrast between the ups and downs in life is greater. On a piece of white cloth, even a small dust particle is clearly seen. Similarly, when the mind becomes more pure, even small jealousy or anger is an irritant. It is unbearable and you have to get rid of it quickly. This is but quite natural.

At the same time, you get the inner strength to endure situations.

When we are joyous with ourselves then nothing from outside can seem boring to us.

If you don't like something then your focus is all the more on it. If you like something then you focus on it. When you're neutral about something, when there is no aversion then there is no focus.

Studying the nature of mind is itself an amazing phenomenon. You will be thrilled knowing and learning more and more about your own mind. When I say mind, I don't mean just mind. I would rather say the consciousness because the mind is one function of the consciousness. The perception is what we call the mind. The perceptible aspect of the consciousness is called mind. The judgmental aspect, the intellect. The study of consciousness is the most difficult. And with time and maturity, everybody gets it.

You should aspire for enlightenment and enlightenment is unconditional happiness, unconditional love and a life in which you are in the driver's seat. You must aspire for enlightenment. Right from when you recognize to aspire anything in life. Go to the highest first and all the good things will come along, you don't have to make an effort for it. When I say you don't have to make an effort, I mean

you don't have to sit and worry about it. When you aspire for the highest, your action will be spontaneous and in the spontaneity you will see things have started falling into place.

When you worry there is a tendency to lose that focus or centredness. It is the same when you are tired or too busy. Self-referral means coming back to yourself, to your centre again and again, – the core value within you.

You should know you have a beautiful mind. The mind is free, it is loving, beautiful, satisfied and not feverish. So when the spirit is centred or your mind is centred, that beauty shines through.

My consciousness is nitnutan (new every moment). First, we get bored with ourselves and then bore others or get bored of others. When we are joyous with ourselves then nothing from outside can seem boring to us.

Wanting enlightenment itself is half done. The rest is a little discipline and you should know that you will get it. It will be given to you. That's why you have the path, the Guru. You will just get it. Shama jali hai tere liye, tujhko kuch nahi karna hai (the candle is lit for you, you don't have to do anything). You don't have to do anything. Just be hollow and empty from inside.

There are so many things to do in the world. Where is the time to live in the past, recollect all the past? Right? The world is new every moment. Go with it. Don't turn back and keep looking back. Move forward.

Enlightenment is the biggest happiness. Why to go after small happiness when the biggest is there? It is not easy to believe in God. God is there – If you experience this then the mind calms down.

Then you find only God is there and I don't exist.

Anything done to uplift your spirit, to make you walk towards the truth that brings up human values within, that connects you to the innermost and outermost is spiritual. Meditation, pranayama, yoga, service, singing, chanting, creating happiness around you are all part of spirituality. If you create misery then that is not spirituality. If you can create joy, it is spiritual.

Blame is what you call that criticism, which you cannot accept. How do you deal with blame? With patience, it needs enormous patience and faith that truth will triumph always, things will get better.

You see changes in yourself that is good enough. Others' can't because they are caught in their own mind. With patience express yourself better. Many times our actions are not aligned with our feelings. Outward action may be rough but you may not feel rough inside. Your feelings have changed, but your actions and expressions have not changed. In most cases, that, is what happens. Then you need to change your expression a little bit.

When you don't expect anything from your friends then you will be centred. You know, when you are friendly some sort of expectation is there, you enjoy being friendly. Stop enjoying being friendly. But be friendly because it's your very nature. Then you will be centred.

Environment is a really serious issue. You should all plant trees, use less refrigeration, and turn to vegetarianism. You know, scientists today say if the whole world stops butchering, the entire greenhouse effect issue will be resolved. One slaughter is equivalent to the cutting of 500 trees, for it releases that much methane. The amount of food used for one animal can be used to feed 400 people. Go veg: stay

healthy and save the planet. It is as simple as that.

Feeling helpless is obviously a sign of weakness, but if with that helplessness prayer arises in you then an unknown, unseen, irrefutable strength comes to you. But you can't force yourself to feel helpless or to pray. It comes automatically.

Nature of devotion is such that you feel longing in its absence. Once you get a glimpse of devotion then its absence causes perturbation in mind. It is not that devotion is absent there but you feel as if it is not there, and you feel restless with this feeling. If we look in the light of knowledge, Saint Narada has said in the Bhakti Sutras that the very indication of devotion is that you experience bliss in its presence and its absence makes you restless. This shows that you have devotion, and consider yourself as lucky when you experience such restlessness in the mind.

Every question is not answered on the spot. Once a couple went to a Master and expressed their wish to ask two questions. The Master said, 'You will get your answers if you do service for two years.' The more precious is the question, the more effort is to be done to get the answer.

Trust in yourself. Have faith in your choice of actions and the path you would be following. If you don't trust yourself, how can you trust the Master? It is enough to have faith in yourself.

A Master or a Guru does not remove the doubt, but He creates more doubts. The more you burn in the fire of doubt, the more strong you come out to be. Truth is never afraid of doubt, and truth can never hide.

There have been so many saints in ancient India like Vishavamitra, Valmiki, Gautama, and you will deprive yourself of knowledge if you start doubting all of him/her.

If you put your attention on the real and authentic, you would doubt the fake. But if all your attention is on the fake, you would start doubting the authentic as well.

The effect of divine energy is such that it transforms all the negative tendencies in the mind. Whatever has been said in the Yogasutras, 'Tat sanidho vair tyaga', is very true – One gets free from the feeling of animosity in the company of truth, in the company of those who practise meditation.

The secret of birth is one of the five secrets. Nature has been very kind that birth has been kept as a secret. Otherwise, you would be living a miserable life remembering all previous incidents that happened in the past lives. But a time will come in your life when your mind would be completely established in the present moment, memory would awake, and you will remember what you were and who you were in your previous births. It is all right if it does not happen with some people.

The whole world is made up of cause and effect. If somebody is rich, that has a reason. If somebody is poor, that also has a reason. But does that mean we don't have any independence of Karma? You definitely have freedom. We have been given discrimination. So, we do have freedom of karma, and also we are bearing fruits of past actions as well. It is like you get some capital from someone. Now, it is up to you what you want to do with it. A poor man can become rich, and a rich can become poor. There are all possibilities. Your karma decided where you were born. But it depends on you where you want to reach.

Vairagya or dispassion is associated with viveka or the power of discrimination. When we were small children, we wanted to have cotton candy or lollipops and toys. As we grew up, these desires

dropped by him/herselves. We became dispassionate about toys, but got attached to something else. In course of time, desires drop effortlessly. When we move ahead with awareness then our attachments drop even faster, with love.

One thing we need to remember is that the whole story will be finished here! All of us will be gone! We will all go under ground. Life will come to an end, right? If we look back and see so many people we once knew are now gone. Those who were with us, they are all finished. More will go. Everybody will go and, one day, we will also be gone. This is the permanent truth, the definite truth in life.

□

Understanding the Significance of Diwali

Diwali means the festival of lights. Each one of you is a light to yourself. This festival is celebrated throughout India, Nepal, Singapore, Malaysia, Sri Lanka, Indonesia, Mauritius, Suriname, Trinidad, and South Africa. People wish one another 'Happy Diwali' and exchange sweets.

During Diwali, we let go of all the past burdens in the mind. Whatever is suppressed in the mind, you light firecrackers and let it go. Like crackers, the past is gone, all burnt out and a fresh new mind begins. This is Diwali.

One candle is not enough. Everyone has to be happy and light up. Everyone has to be happy and wise. The light of wisdom is lit. Symbolically, we will light the light of wisdom and celebrate today.

The Diwali message is: Let go of the past. Celebrate life with wisdom. Without wisdom it is not true celebration at all. The wisdom is in knowing that the divinity is with me.

Today is the day that you also look at all the wealth you have. You remember you have so much wealth and feel the abundance. Otherwise, the mind is always in the space of lack, 'Oh! This is not there, that is not there, sorry for this, sorry for that.' From lack, move on to abundance. The ancient custom is to put in front of you all the gold and silver coins. You bring all your wealth in front of you and say, 'Look, God has given me all this. I am so thankful!'

The Bible says, 'Those who have more will be given to him/her; those who do not have, whatever little they have will also be taken away.' Feeling that abundance, you recognize you have been given plenty.

Then we do Laxmi Pooja. The goddess of wealth and prosperity is worshipped, and Lord Ganesh – that impulse of consciousness

that removes all the obstacles in our path to happiness – that chanting is done today.

For each country we will light one lamp. There are 27 countries in Europe. We will light one lamp for each country. Then we will meditate for a few minutes. When we meditate, we thank the Universal spirit, power for giving us in abundance. We also pray for more so that we may serve more. Yes?

Gold and silver are all just outer symbols. The real wealth is deep within us. There is so much love, peace and joy. What more wealth do you need than this? Wisdom is the real wealth. Your character, your peace and confidence are the real wealth.

When you move with a connection to the divinity there is nothing that is richer than this. That rich feeling comes inside you when you feel connected to the divinity, connected to the infinite. When the wave remembers that it is connected to the ocean, that it is part of the ocean, that strength is enormous!

Lord Krishna tells Arjuna that one who is dear to me is who doesn't hate anybody, who doesn't have any ego – I, I, me. One who is calm in success or failure. Whatever he gets – sorrow or happiness – he takes it all with a smile.

Every child is born with spiritual knowledge but when you grow up, you start losing that. A yogi is becoming a child again, getting in touch with your pure essence.

The teacher gives you the problem and he wants you to find a solution to the problem. In schools and colleges, you are not given solutions and asked to find problems to him/her. A teacher's job is to create confusion so that you may exercise your intellect, your mind, your intuition and your inner voice to see and come up with a solution.

Only a calm mind can come up with collective thoughts. Disturbed and chaotic mind will give rise to chaotic thoughts only and chaotic thoughts are coming in abundance. How to streamline the thoughts is an art in itself, the art of silence? How can you do it? With meditation, the mind becomes calm and collective, thoughts become focused, meaningful and purposeful.

The great Indian Saint Kabir has said that 'Keep someone who criticizes you close by, that will keep your house, your mind clean – without soap and water.' Like you need soap and water to keep your body clean, like that one who blames you, you should keep close by. If everybody around keeps praising you, he/she may not keep all the facts in front of you. Someone who is criticizing you, will show you your pitfalls. Welcome criticism, anybody who criticizes you, welcome that. Don't shy away from criticism. You should be able to give constructive criticism and also take criticism. That is the strength. And there is no good critique or bad critique. Keep him/her near by means that don't run away from critique, don't stop talking to him/her. You stop talking with someone who criticizes you. Yesterday if somebody criticized you, you talk to him/her normally today. Don't shun him/her.

The universe is so mysterious. Everything is mysterious. We shouldn't try to understand everything. Just leave the mystery. The whole knowledge is to move from an ugly 'I don't know, don't ask me' to a beautiful 'Wow, I don't know.'

When you're meditating, we're doing so much good to society, to the world around. It generates and releases positive ions in the environment and it is the positive ions that affect thinking, mind, spirit and body, the environment in the universe. It is very important, very precious – not only for us, but also for the world around.

□

Understanding the Benefits of Vegetarianism

There are several angles to it. Karma means the latent impression in a substance and how your body matches.

Suppose a lion hunts a deer and eats the deer; the lion does not get the karma. A cat eats a mouse; the cat does not get the karma of the mouse. All these animals are designed to prey and eat. However, if you see the human physiology, it is more akin to herbivores. There is a substance called tannin in our saliva which is present only in the cow, elephant, horse, goat – in all the herbivorous animals. This indicates that the human saliva is made for herbivorous animals.

Secondly, the human intestine is so long – six feet. This is not present in a lion, tiger or dog but it is present in all herbivores. If you look at the physiology of human beings, we don't have canine teeth. All herbivorous animals don't have canine teeth. Only the carnivorous animals do.

If you look at these aspects, physiologically our system is more akin to vegetarianism. So in that sense, we say, when you eat a vegetarian diet, you don't get the karma of it. If you eat anything that is not aligning with your body – like if an elephant eats an egg or if you feed a cow with meat then the cow will get the karma.

What is karma? Karma is the impression which is against the nature that can produce some change in the consciousness. It can be harmful to the consciousness.

Similarly, when we are exposed to radiation, which we are not supposed to, we get diseases. That means, we acquire those karma. Karma means the strongest impressions on the nervous system which is not all the time necessarily desirable.

If you have drugs, you have drug karma and the karma of the drug on the nervous system is so huge that after some time, you can't stop the drug. Then your body craves for it. Your body distorts. You go through so much of pain and suffering. It needs lot of de-programming to come out of drug addiction. It is the same for alcohol.

Food is not that strong. Yet, our system is made for herbivores, especially if you want to go more subtle in your mind and in your consciousness.

All top scientists, many achievers are vegetarians. It naturally happens. Your system wants only that. That means they are in tune with Nature. That's all. It's not that those who are not vegetarian are not good. No, they are as good as you are. But their consciousness is much better if they tune him/herselves to Nature.

□

Understanding Karma

Karma is the impression in the consciousness. The impression draws similar situations, events and actions. So karma has three things: One is the latent karma – it is karma as an impression; Karma as an action; and Karma as a result.

You look at a banana. Looking at a banana is a karma. It is an action, and you want to eat it because you know that you have eaten it before. That is the impression of the banana. It is karma as an impression. Then you crave for it. That is a result of it. That's also karma. Looking at it, wanting to have it, craving for it, and, in fact, really eating it is also karma.

Too much dreaming, too much wanting to do, this has all caused the insomnia. I want nothing, I do nothing – keep these two things in mind. You will fall asleep like a baby.

There is a Universal Power that is inside of me, outside of me, and everywhere in the universe. That power is responsible for everything in the universe. All the diverse creation is because of this power and that power cares for me. Some people call it God, some call it something else. But it does not matter what one calls it. There is a power, there is a spirit. That is so compassionate, and it is with me and will help me!

□

Understanding Spiritual Evolution

You have always thought of God as a father, up in the heavens somewhere. But can you see God as a child? When you see God as a father, you will want to demand and take from Him. But when you see God as a child, you have no demands. God is the very core of your existence. You are pregnant with God. You have to take care of your pregnancy and deliver this Child into the world. God is your child who clings onto you like a baby till you grow old and die. This child clings on to you crying for nourishment. Sadhana, Satsang and Seva are the nourishment.

It is difficult to see God as formless and it is difficult to see God as form. The formless is so abstract and God in a form appears to be too limited. So some people prefer to be atheists. But atheism is not a reality, it is just a matter of convenience.

When you have a spirit of inquiry, or are in search of truth, atheism falls apart. With a spirit of inquiry, you cannot deny something which you have not disproved. An atheist denies God without first disproving it. In order to disprove God, you must have enormous knowledge. And when you have enormous knowledge, you cannot disprove God. For one to say that something does not exist, one should know about the whole universe. So you can never be 100 per cent atheist. An atheist is only a believer who is sleeping. In fact an atheist is someone who has a concept of God. For a person to say, I don't believe in anything, means he must believe in himself so he may believe in himself about whom he does not even know.

An atheist can never be sincere because sincerity needs depth and an atheist refuses to go to the depths. Because the deeper he goes, he finds a void, a field of all possibilities he has to accept that there are many secrets he does not know. He would then need to

acknowledge his ignorance, which he refuses to do, because the moment he is sincere, he seriously starts doubting his atheism.

A doubt-free atheist is next to impossible So you can never be a sincere and doubt-free atheist. When the atheist realises his ignorance, what does he do? Where does he go? Does he go to a Guru? What does a Guru do to him? Atheism is when one does not believe either in values or in the abstract. When an atheist comes to the guru, what happens? You start experiencing your own form and discover that you are indeed formless, hollow and empty. And this abstract non-form in you becomes more and more concrete.

The guru makes the abstract more real and what you thought as solid appears to be more unreal. Sensitivity and subtlety dawns. Perception of love, not as an emotion, but as the substratum of existence becomes evident. The formless spirit shines through every form in creation and the mystery of life deepens, shattering the atheism. Then the journey begins and it has four stages.

The first stage is Saarupya (to see the formless in the form) i.e. seeing God in all the forms. Often, one feels more comfortable seeing God as formless, rather than with a form, because with a form, one feels a distance, a duality, a fear of rejection and other limitations.

In life all our interactions are with the form, other than in deep sleep and in Samadhi. And, if you do not see God in the form, then the waking part of life remains devoid of the Divine. All those who accept God to be formless use symbols, and perhaps love the symbols more than God Himself. If God comes and tells a Christian to leave the cross or a Muslim to drop the crescent, perhaps he may not do it. To begin with, loving the formless is possible only through forms.

The second stage is Saamipya (closeness) i.e. feeling absolutely close to the form you have chosen and reaching out to the formless. This leads to a sense of intimacy with the whole of creation. In this stage, one overcomes the fear of rejection and other fears. But this is time and space bound.

The third stage is Saanidhya, i.e. feeling the presence of the Divine by which you transcend the limitations of time and space.

Then the final stage is Saayujya, i.e. when you are firmly

entrenched with the Divine. It is then that you realise you are one with the Divine. There is a total merging with the Beloved and all duality disappears.

Take care of your God. Atheists lurk around the corner. Doubts, disbelief and ignorance are the atheists in your mind so you had better take care.

□

Understanding the True Essence of Shiva and Shivratri

Let us understand a little about the Shiva tattva. Only a little can be known. The intellect has to be content and finer feelings awakened. Both scientific understanding and spiritual wisdom are necessary to bring this contentment, that is holistic and complete. There is no need to go on long pilgrimages to find the Divine. If you don't find God here, where you are, then it is not possible anywhere else. Where the mind dissolves, Shiva is there. Be established wherever you are. The moment you are established, centred, you see that there is Divinity present everywhere. This is meditation. One of the names of Lord Shiva is Virupaksha – meaning one who is formless yet sees all. We know that there is air all around us and we can feel the air as well. What if the air also starts feeling you? Space is all around us; we identify space. What if space also recognizes and feels your presence? This happens. Only we don't know it. Scientists know this and they call it the theory of relativity. The one who sees and that which is seen are both affected when seen. The Divine is all around you and is seeing you. He doesn't have a form. He is the formless core of existence and the goal. He is the seer, sight and the scene. This formless Divinity is Shiva. To wake up and experience this Shiva tattva is Shivratri.

Usually when there is celebration, awareness is lost. Deep rest in celebration with awareness is Shivratri. When you face some problem, you become aware and alert. We are at rest when everything is well; on Shivratri we rest with awareness. It is said that a yogi remains awake when everybody else is sleeping. For a yogi, every day is Shivratri. Lord Shiva is beautifully explained in a verse by Adi Shankaracharya.

Adyantahinam – One without a beginning, or end. Sarvada – He is the Bholenath (innocent ruler of all) who is present everywhere all the time. We think Shiva is somewhere else sitting with a snake around his neck. Shiva is one in whom everything has taken birth, who encompasses everything right this moment, and in whom everything in creation dissolves. Every form you see in this creation is all his form.

He permeates the entire creation. He is never born and has no end. He is eternal.

He is the fourth state of consciousness, the turiya avasta, the meditative state that is beyond the waking, deep sleep and dream state.

He is the non-dual consciousness that is present everywhere. That's why to do Shiva pooja, you have to dissolve in Shiva yourself. Being Shiva, you do Shiva pooja. Chidananda rupa – He is the consciousness, that is pure bliss.

Tapo yoga gamya – One who can be known through tapa and yoga. The Shiva tattva can be experienced in the knowledge of the Vedas. The state of Shivoham (I am Shiva), Shiva kevaloham (there is only Shiva) is attained. Shivratri is the day to experience a wave of joy and contentment. Without yoga, Shiva can't be experienced. Yoga doesn't mean only asanas (physical postures), but that experience of Shiva tattva which happens with meditation, pranayama… when that 'WOW' happens from within.

The word Shambo has come from the same source – to realize how beautiful the Divine is, the creation and the Self is! It is a miracle how the same consciousness is present in every being in this creation! There is no other miracle greater than this. How did this One become so many? This tradition (of Shivratri) of moving from many to one is so unique. Yoga and meditation is necessary for that. Without meditation, the mind is not calmed. On the occasion of Shivratri meditation, bhajans are all part of the celebration. Everyone participates with a full heart. Everyone should sing. Shiva is the cause of all causes. Because of which everything is there – the tree growing, the sun rising, the wind blowing... The reason for everything happening is Shiva – because of whom everything happens and without whom,

nothing happens. Panchmukha, Panchtattva – There are five faces to Shiva – Water, Air, Earth, Fire and Space. Understanding these five elements is tattva gyana (knowledge of the five elements). And then Shiva is worshipped as Ashtamurti (eight forms) – Mind, Memory, Ego are also included. This is both the form and formless aspect of Shiva. Worshipping Shiva is dissolving in the Shiv tattva and then wishing for something good. What to wish for? Wish with a liberal heart for the Universal good, nobody should be unhappy in the world. 'Sarve janah sukhino bhavantu.' And make one sankalpa on this occasion. It is something which comes to you again and again like your breath, like your heartbeat. And when you surrender such a sankalpa to the Divine, it will definitely come true.

We also worship Nature. Divinity permeates everything in this Earth. Pooja is not complete without honouring trees, mountains, rivers, the earth and the people living on the earth. Honouring everyone is dakshina. Da means to give and dakshina means giving something that will cleanse us of all impurities. Offering with which all your sins vanish. No pooja is complete without dakshina. When we act in society with skill and are free from the distortions of the mind, all negative tendencies like anger, worries, sorrow are destroyed. I will say give your tensions, worries and sorrows as dakshina. And how does that happen? With sadhana (spiritual practices), seva (service) and satsang (company of the truth).

Ride the boat of the intellect to dissolve in the ocean of finer feelings and faith.

The guru makes the abstract more real and what you thought as solid appears to be more unreal. Sensitivity and subtlety dawns. Perception of love, not as an emotion, but as the substratum of existence becomes evident. The formless spirit shines through every form in creation and the mystery of life deepens, shattering the atheism. Then the journey begins!

Understanding Human Connection with Nature

The realities explored in science and spirituality are often assumed to be unrelated to one another. Both find their basis in a spirit of inquiry. Modern science is objective analysis, while spirituality is subjective understanding. Science explores the outer world with a series of questions beginning with the basic query, 'What is this? What is this world all about,' while spirituality begins with the question, 'Who am I?'

In the ancient world, these two forms of knowledge were not in conflict, but were understood to have a deep and subtle connection. Man's knowledge of himself complemented his understanding of the universe and formed the basis for a strong and healthy relationship to the creation in which he lived. It is the disconnection between these two types of knowledge which is causing many of the challenges that we face as a global community today.

Ancient wisdom describes human beings as having five layers of experience – the environment, the physical body, the mind, the intuition and our self or spirit.

Our connection with the environment is our first level of experience, and one of the most important. If our environment is clean and positive, it has a positive impact on all the other layers of our existence. As a result, they come into balance and we experience a greater sense of peace and connection within ourselves and with others around us.

An intimate relationship with the environment is built into the human psyche. Historically Nature, mountains, rivers, trees, the sun, the moon have always been honoured in ancient cultures. It's only

when we start moving away from our connection to Nature and ourselves, that we begin polluting and destroying the environment. We need to revive these attitudes that foster our connection with Nature.

Today we live in a world where many have become greedy and want to make quick profits and achieve quick results. Their actions disrupt the ecological balance, and not only pollute the physical environment, but also stimulate negative emotions on a subtle level, within him/herselves and also in those around him/her. These negative energies expanded and compounded again and again are the root cause of much of the violence and misery in this world.

Most wars and conflicts are triggered by such feelings, and result in damage to the environment, which then takes a long time to restore and repair. We need to attend to the human psyche which is the root cause of pollution, both physical and emotional. If compassion and care are kindled within ourselves, they will form the basis for a deeper connection to, and care for both others and the environment.

In ancient times, if a person cut one tree, he planted five in return. The ancient people did not wash clothes in holy rivers; only ashes from cremation were submerged in the river so that everything dissolved might go back into Nature. We need to revive traditional practices of honouring and conserving Nature.

Nature has its own means of balance. If you observe nature, you will see that the five elements which form its basis are opposed to one another. Water destroys fire; fire destroys air. Then there are so many species in Nature – birds, reptiles, mammals; all these different species are hostile towards one another, and yet Nature balances him/her out. We need to learn from Nature how to balance opposing forces, within ourselves and in the world around us.

Above all, we need to be able to experience our world with an open mind that is free from stress, and from that place we need to create the means of protecting our beautiful planet earth. For this to happen, human consciousness must rise above greed and exploitation. Spirituality, the experience of one's own nature, deep within, provides the key to this vital relationship with oneself, with others and with our environment. This connection to our own essential nature eliminates negative emotions, elevates one's consciousness and creates a spirit of care and commitment for the whole planet.

What would help to elevate our consciousness and deepen our connection? Here are a few basic and effective pointers:

A proper diet. Our food influences our mind. The Jain tradition has done much research on the effect of food on the mind. Ayurveda and Chinese systems and many other native systems the world over have recognized the effect of food on the psyche. Modern science confirms that food can have a direct bearing on our emotions. Emotionally disturbed children tend to eat more and suffer from obesity. A properly balanced diet has a positive impact on our emotions and thereby on our consciousness.

Light to moderate exercise.

Panchkarma. In the ancient medical system of Ayurveda, there is a process of internal cleansing called panchkarma that involves massages, a prescribed diet and cleansing. This has helped thousands of people to come out of stress and behavioural disorders and is also a curative for many illnesses.

Yoga, pranayama and meditation. These are extremely vital to induce a sense of respect for one's own body and the environment. They help to maintain a toxin-free system and thereby reduce the occurrence of emotional disturbances.

Music and dance. These can bring rhythm and harmony in the body-mind complex; especially music that is not too loud and violent. Music that is soothing and creates a gentle sway and rhythm in one's system, like folk and classical music.

Nature. Spending time in Nature, observing silence and engaging in prayer is very congenial for helping us to reflect on our own mind.

Last but not the least: **Service to the less fortunate.**

Our voices should be strong. The voice of truth and religion is weak. When the voice of violence is strong, it creates trouble. When the voice of love is strong and the voice of violence is weak, that is satyayuga (the age of truth). The voice of Rama should be stronger

than Ravana's. Only then can he win. It is the same with Lord Krishna.

It is when life feels like a struggle that we must focus on knowledge. Even Arjuna was not first told to fight. He was told to be in knowledge and meditation. Only then should we work. Always be in knowledge and then work.

To get knowledge we don't need to go to the Himalayas. Knowledge can come even in the activities of everyday life. Wanting perfection in work sometimes creates anger. If somebody does something wrong, it can create anger.

There are three types of perfection:

Perfection in mind is keeping our mind in peace.

Perfection in speech is to speak only when needed. No need to get into fights.

Perfection in action. Perfection in action is not 100 per cent possible.

However, perfection in mind and speech can be obtained by sadhana (spiritual practices), seva (service) and satsang (music and meditation). Once our mind and speech are perfect, work will also become perfect automatically.

The culture of India is to accommodate everyone. Nobody is different. We have made everybody our own. For instance, the Guru Granth Sahib expresses Brahmagyan in a simple language. This is the special aspect of India. We should not keep this knowledge within us. We should share so that everybody may get the benefit. This is also important.

People often ask, 'Why do we pray to so many gods and goddesses?' The Paramatma (the Divine) is one, yet called by different names. Just as with the same flour, we may make noodles sometimes and on another occasion, samosa (an Indian snack) or something else. It is still all the same flour. In the same way, it is the same Paramatma that we evoke through different names, forms and colours.

The meaning of aarti is complete happiness. Only when our life's radiance is around God, do we get complete happiness. We should dive into the meaning of all rituals and then we will be happy and make others happy. We have to get rid of unhappiness. We all should do pranayama. We should focus on our breath every day for 10 minutes or so. This is called pranayama and kriya. Through this, people can experience bliss. To be in bliss is total rest. The kriya also helps to maintain health as well as purifies the mind, intellect and emotions. It helps us to come out of our guilt and be in the present moment.

Where all are happy, God comes. When the mind is happy our work gets done and we are able to bless others to heal him/herselves. All powers are hidden within the Self. Atma gyan (Self-knowledge) will bring these out. If you bless people, everything will manifest. If you have a cell phone but don't dial the number, will that work? You have to connect to yourself, prakriti (your nature), atma and paramatma. Then everything will manifest.

Thirty minutes of meditation will make you look brighter. We should all meditate for thirty minutes every day. We should all go to temple and sit with our eyes closed for a few minutes. Do not leave a temple without meditating.

We have got everything and we are sitting here, keeping our mind free, clean and pure. Our only condition is you have to give up all your tension, stress, worries, pain. All these you must give up here and go home with a smile. Life is to be lived with happiness. We should not live life with sadness nor make others sad. Give up every unhappiness here. I am here only to remind you that God is there and He is your very own.

You have already broken it the moment you realize the pattern.

You realize it is your own mind's making and that it has happened over and over again. This realization will come in its own time. And when this happens, be happy and grateful. Imagine where you were five or ten years back. How have you changed? How much better it has become since then. Put your attention on this. The more we are grateful, the more grace we will have in our life.

You assume that you have devotion. Don't strive to have devotion. We should assume that we have love and devotion in us. When you believe in this, the devotion in you enhances. When you think you don't have devotion at all, it wouldn't manifest.

Meditation is when you are awake as well as relaxed.

You don't know anything in deep sleep. Only after you have waken up, you get to know that you were sleeping. And a dream is a dream. The experiences that you already have had, when those reflect again in your mind, your consciousness; that is dream.

If that is very much needed by you, you would not be able to go without praying. And have this faith that God will give you what you need.

Longing and love are the two sides of the same coin. You can't say, 'I love you but I don't long for you.' And it is impossible to long for someone without having love. That is why it is said: 'RadheShyam'. Radha is longing and Shyam is love. RadheShyam (longing and love) go together in life.

Prana is present in everything. In fact, we are floating in air, in prana, an ocean of prana. When the unit of expression varies, it makes a difference. Stones have got one unit of prana. Water has got two units of prana. Fire has got three units of prana. Air has got four

units of prana. Plants have got five units of prana. Animals have got six units of prana. Human beings are capable of holding from seven to sixteen units of prana. The expression of prana is the whole universe. When prana is lower than one, that's when you feel depressed. When prana goes further low then you feel suicidal. When prana is normal, you feel normal. When prana is higher, you feel enthusiastic. When prana is very high, you feel energetic and blissful. That is why when people are depressed (low) just giving counselling doesn't work; what needs to be done is to raise the level of prana. When prana is high, there is joy, vibrancy, understanding. When prana is low then the mind starts complaining. Depression, lethargy, suicidal tendencies arise. All is play and display of prana.

Youth are bored and it's their fortune. If they were satisfied then growth would have stopped. When they are bored then the quest comes in him/her. They are not satisfied with the things available around. And this is the stage when they can take a step to look within, a leap in their inner journey, a step towards spirituality. An interest in higher growth gets kindled, when you are bored with things around. When you find the source of joy within then obviously everything around is also reflecting the same source of joy then you find interest in everything. Continuous bombardment of senses by stimuli can cause inertia. Inertia is boredom is a form of boredom. When prana level goes up, you move from inertia to enthusiasm.

The most unreliable thing you have is your own mind because you don't know what it likes and when it doesn't like that. That is why bringing mind to its source is so important. Its centredness is the most important thing in spiritual evolution. Understanding what is transient and what is permanent; what brings you permanent joy; and what causes temporary convenience and long-term misery; what causes temporary discomfort and permanent joy; and what causes long-term discomfort. That is what is called viveka, discrimination, wisdom – knowing this from that.

□

Understanding Significance of 33 Crore Devas

Crore, koti means types. 33 Crore means 33 types of Divine impulses. In our body also, there are 33 types of divine impulses. There are 33 types of genes in our body. A particular type makes the eye, a particular type makes the nose, like that a particular type makes eardrums, hair, nails. All these are made up from a particular type of gene which are of 33 different types.

Like this, there are 33 rays of Divinity. There is one light, one God, one Parmatma, yet there are 33 aspects. Devas are the 33 different aspects of Divinity. Here, crore is not referred to as a number. The Divine has no form but ancient saints have said you can adore Him in any form or name. All the thousand names belong to God only. This is very very deep science or deep knowledge. It's amazing. When you go deeper into this then you feel the 'wow'. People, who have written this, have discovered this, have simply stupendous knowledge. The universe is not so simple. It's very complex. Modern physics also says that the deeper and deeper you go, there are so many different type of particles. So the universe is diverse. The Divinity which manages, rules, and has made this diverse universe is devta.

The English name, David, is a Sanskrit word. Dev + vid, dev means Divinity, vid means to know. David means one who knows Divinity. Divinity is not somewhere up in heaven. It is present in the world, universe, everywhere. And it has to be realized when the mind is calm, serene and settled in our heart and when the emotion and intellect merge into a serene blend in silence then you are able to perceive the subtle reality of the universe and, that is, devta.

That which is born from purnata (fullness) is pooja. When gratitude is overwhelming, the throat chokes in gratitude then whatever action you perform in such a state is pooja. We surrender everything – that bhavana (feeling) is pooja.

It is better to forget bad things and it is good to remember good things. Both together are life; but we forget this and remember all the negative things. It is important to remember what you hear in satsang. Forgetting other people's mistakes is important. Remembering not to repeat our mistakes is important. Remembering lessons from others' mistakes is also important.

Ashwamedha means to purify. Shwa means that which is the past or future. Ashwa means that which is present and medha means cleansing. Ashwamedha is when the cleansing of the mind and buddhi (intellect) happens in the present moment. Keep the mind/buddhi (intellect) in the present moment.

Knowing of this 'I' can lead to a state of devotion, of love. It is spontaneous. There is no need for surrender, because it is already there. It does not have to mean a painful part of the ego. It is knowing that everything belongs to the divine, the thorn as well as the rose belong to the divine. What happens when you surrender? A permanent peace dawns in you, a smile that no one can take away from you.

Adi Shankaracharya said that the definition of truth is that which is untouched by time. It is that which stayed the same yesterday, stays the same today and shall be the same tomorrow. So going by this definition, body and mind are not the truth. Truth is the substratum of creation. There is something at the core of our being that is not changing and that is the Absolute Truth. That's why even when you become old, you don't feel you have become old. Somewhere we

know that something in us will not die at all.

The problem arises when you carry money not only in your pocket but in your head as well. Also, what is the use of thinking about it all the time if your pockets are empty? Money is the means and not an end in itself. Have faith that you will get whatever money you need. Put in your effort and move forward with this conviction. Also, out of the money you earn, 2-3% should be spent for others. We call it dhana-shuddhi (purification of wealth).

In Sanskrit, there is a word anna-shuddhi (purification of grains). It prescribes adding ghee (clarified butter) to rice. If you eat rice alone, it is not so good for your body as the sugar level in your blood suddenly increases. By adding just a little bit of clarified butter (ghee), the process of converting the starch into sugar is slowed down. So the digestion process becomes slower and you are less prone to diabetes. So we say rice gets purified when we add ghee to it. Similarly, money gets purified when we contribute to those in need.

Your body, mind, consciousness are all made up of truth, love, beauty and peace. Take it for granted that you love yourself. Nobody can afford to love oneself because you are love. That's just an illusion if it appears that you don't love yourself.

If the technology of cell phones can reach everywhere in the world, why would techniques wisdom that make people happy and peaceful not reach every home? They definitely will. We should have a vision to do something that appears impossible and make it possible. It is my habit and hobby!

Why do you want to be disciplined? It will make you happier. It will improve your fitness and health. So it is the love for being in shape or the fear of becoming unhealthy that will keep you disciplined. Love, fear and greed bring discipline.

When your intention and attention are there, manifestation happens. If your intention is not there, it will not work. Sudarshan Kriya works because there is an intention behind it. For anything to work, you must have intention and attention. Then manifestation happens.

When the left nostril is active then the right brain is active, and vice-versa. The right brain is music. The left brain is logic. So those who have the right nostril active would understand me better. If both are active you are in meditation. However if only the right nostril is active, no meditation happens. Your state changes every time you open and close your eyes. After food, the right nostril should dominate. When the right nostril functions the metabolism is 50 per cent higher. When the left is functioning, our metabolism is much slower.

Active nostrils change because they live in an ocean of prana (energy). Breath moves from right to left nostril depending on the situation. If you are driving around a church, temple or any place of worship, both nostrils will become active. The prana of both the body and spirit is up in those places. When people are in full devotion in a place of worship, this happens. When you meet a spiritual guide, both your nostrils will become active. When you meet a spiritual person, your own voice will tell you.

Be in the 'now'. Desire is wanting to be happy tomorrow. Be happy and joyful now. Like children, if you ask him/her what they want, they will say nothing. Because they are happy with 'now'.

Negative thoughts are due to three reasons. If your blood circulation is not good, if the lymphatic system is not OK or if bowel movement is irregular. In all these cases, negative thoughts are likely. You can go on a fruit diet and cleanse your intestines. Then, pranayama will help. Take Triphala (an ayurvedic supplement) for a few days. Do yoga, pranayama and meditation. You will definitely find a

difference. Group sadhana (practice) will also help.

It makes you feel better when you release the tears. The impressions go him/herselves. You don't need any effort to make yourself close to God. God is the closest thing to you. There is no escape from God! However you are, good or bad, God is all around you. Like there is air all around you. Whether you are awake or asleep, air is all around. When you feel hot, you stand in front of the fan. The fan is just blowing the air, which is already there. Satsang is like a fan. The Master is like a fan. Only then do you feel the blow of the air.

De-link the pain from the memory. But if you put effort in trying to do that, you bring the memory back. However, in meditation, you feel the pain as a sensation and not as connected to an event. In the Art of Silence Course, during the Hollow and Empty Meditation, you observe pain as a sensation. The very first experience of life was pain, coming out of our mother's womb through such a small passage. Before that you were in bliss. You didn't even need to eat. Then suddenly the water got drained and you came out crying. Have you noticed the expression on a newborn's face? It is as though he/she came out from ten hours of hard work! The first experience is that of pain. Then the child looks into the mother's eyes, and then the mother experiences the love.

Don't see pain as an event.

Care for Nature, like native communities worship Nature. Honour the environment. In a place in India if you cut one tree, you have to promise you will plant five of the same kind within the next forty days. There is a whole ritual in which one who is cutting the tree speaks to it, telling it that after cutting it will be useful to us. We must care for Nature, not exploit it.

The whole of life is a game to be played. It is not a struggle. Nothing can destroy you. You are a drop of immortality, a drop of something eternal. Your spirit is eternal. And it is all right if this does not ring a bell right now. I will just say what I know and some day you might authenticate it. Do not be afraid of anything. We have no choice.

When you are stuck in concepts, you are in the box. It is when you get an experience that you can come out of the box.

The year 2012 is a fascination. It has become such a sensation. No news is good news till it has become a sensation. We will have more work to do. People will become more spiritual. It will become a necessity and not merely a fashion. The Golden Age is already here.

Many things can be said without words. Some things can't be said with words and some cannot be said even without words. Even if you say, you may not grasp it.

You are so fortunate. Remember these words when you go home. You are very fortunate. You are so amazing and beautiful. Remember this knowledge. Spread joy and smiles. Lessen worry and bring more joy in everyone's lives. You do this job and let the Divine take care of you. Smile at everyone.

Whatever intention you put, that will manifest. Do not label yourself. There should be no 'always'. Accept that you are unaware of your own potentiality. You may think you always have some difficulty, but thinking so is what points the intention in a negative direction. Just know that whatever you want will happen.

The whole essence of the Gita is to act without being attached to the action. It's all about yoga, not about war but your attitude. When you are faced with a situation like war, how do you manage yourself? The worst situation in life is when you have to face a war

and when you have to fight not with an enemy, but with some of your own people. When you have to fight with your own brothers and sisters, how do you handle the situation? It's easy to fight a war with an enemy, someone you don't like. But fighting with someone who is part of your own family is the worst thing.

If you can manage your mind in the worst scenario then you can manage yourself in any situation. Given the extreme example of how you can manage the mind, the consciousness, yourself, that's the whole essence of the Gita, not the war. Skill in action is yoga.

A similar knowledge was taught by Ashtavakra, in the palace. When your spirit is very high and you want liberation, that was Ashtavakra's state. And when your spirit is so low, totally desperate, completely broken and depressed, that was Arjuna's state. At that time, the same knowledge of the Self was given to him in the Bhagavad Gita.

The nature of love is such that it always feels it is not enough, not sufficient. In love, you will never feel that's it, enough is enough. When you are in love, you think you should do more, give more and love more. That sense of wanting more, that sense of in-completion. That's why love is infinite. Infinite has no end, no boundary – more and more, never bored. Boredom means boundary.

Angels are so filled with good intention, they are very benevolent. They do exist, not just in the physical bodies sitting here, but there are others in the ethereal bodies too.

Spiritual blossoming simply means blossoming in life in all dimensions – being happy, at ease with yourself and with everybody around you.

When there is boredom, there will be frustration also; they are twins. But if they dominate your life, that is misery. And if they just come as a fleeting moment and touches you and passes away, if they are like salt in your life, it's okay. It adds taste. But if the salt is taken from a meal, you have trouble.

If you want to grow in Divine Love, you have to drop the pride and all the artificial walls that we build between ourselves and others. Through these walls, we keep judging others, and we think others are judging us.

An uncommitted mind is miserable. A committed mind may at times experience rough weather but it will reap the fruits of its toil.

The ultimate purpose of life is to be of service.

The sattvic intellect is one that just does the job joyfully and is unmindful of the results. Let things happen or not happen – either way, the sattric intellect doesn't lose its enthusiasm.

Abundance is a state of mind within you. If you just look at 'lack', the lack increases in life. See what you have, and then abundance increases.

Faith is realizing that you always get what you need. Faith is giving the Divine a chance to act.

Whatever feeling is there in you at the moment, be with it one hundred per cent. Share it with the Divine.

Love is that phenomenon of dissolving, disappearing, merging, becoming one with the infinite. Love is that phenomenon of total letting go.

□

Golden Tips for Parents

Know how to ride a horse. When you sit on a horseback, you must move with it. You have to rock with the motion, otherwise your back will hurt. Parents have to rock. You have to swing with him/her, know him/her and gently guide. Sometimes you tighten the reins, sometimes loosen. It is the same with kids. Put your foot down sometimes, but also give him/her freedom.

Everything in the universe is moving from one level of perfection to another level. Milk is perfect and when it turns into yogurt, yogurt is perfect. You take out cream from yogurt, and that is perfect, and then you make butter, and that is also perfect. This is one way of looking at it. The other side of looking at it is, the milk got spoilt and you make cheese out of it. When yogurt got spoilt, it became imperfect and you took butter out of it. This is another way to look at it. It all depends on how you look at it. It's imperfection that gives value to perfection. How can you call something perfect? Because there is something which is not perfect. So, the existence of something which is not perfect is absolutely essential to understand something that is perfect. So, the imperfect makes the perfect, perfect!

Mind is energy which is all over the body. See, every cell in your body is emitting some energy and the totality of all that energy around you is what you call the mind. Mind is not present at some point in the brain, but mind is all over the body.

You know, a person has phantom hand, that means he really doesn't have a hand, but he feels he has a hand and he feels sensations like itching or paining in that hand. The person who has lost his

hand or leg in a war or accident, later sometimes, he feels he has a phantom hand or a leg. Though, he doesn't have it physically. That explains or gives a clue that the mind is not just in one spot, it is all around the body. The aura of body is mind. We think that the mind is inside the body; it is the other way around – Body is inside the mind. Body is like the wick of the candle and the mind is like the glow all around.

You make the destiny. What you did yesterday is a tomorrow's destiny, and what you do now is destiny day after.

The first step to fun is relaxation. What tires you is anxiety and ambition for tomorrow. The anger and hatred of yesterday are also clogging our mind. In the same way feverishness pulls down our enthusiasm. In deep relaxation, you will find everything funny. Life becomes a game!

Understanding the Importance of Guru Poornima

Among the 12-13 full moons in a year the vaishakha full moon is dedicated to (his birth and enlightenment); the jyeshtha full moon to mother earth and the aashadha full moon is dedicated to the memory of masters. This is Guru Poornima.

It is the day when the disciple wakes up in his fullness and in the wakefulness he can't be but grateful. This gratitude is not of dwaita (you and me), but of advaita. It is not a river moving from somewhere to somewhere, but is the ocean moving within itself. So, gratefulness on Guru Poornima symbolizes that fullness.

The purpose of the Guru Poornima celebration is to turn back and review and see in this last one year how much one has progressed in life. For a seeker, Guru Poornima is a day of significance, is a day of New Year. It is the day to review one's progress on the spiritual path and renew one's determination and focus on the goal, and to resolve what one wants to do in the coming year. As the full moon rises and sets, the tears of gratitude arise and repose into the vastness of one's own self.

You know, our body has millions of cells, and each cell has its own life. Many cells are being born every day and many are dying. So, you are a moving town. So many cities are on planet Earth and planet Earth is revolving and moving around the Sun. The same way, there are so many cells and so many living beings inside you and you are moving around. You are a moving township. Like in a beehive, there are so many bees which come and sit, but there is one queen bee. If the queen bee goes away, every other bee goes away. In the same way, there is an atom in our body, the queen bee. If that is not there, everything else goes away. Locate in that, in that tiniest of the tiny atom, the atma or the self. It is everywhere yet nowhere. That is the queen bee and that is what you are. That is what the Divine is, and that is the Guru principle. Like there is fatherhood, motherhood, there is Guru-hood as well. You all have to play Guru-hood at least to somebody. You do play, you keep giving advice and guiding people consciously or unconsciously, and give him/her love and care. But do it with 100 per cent without expecting anything in return. That is living the Guru-hood, living the self. There is no difference between the Divine, you and the Guru Principle. It is all coming to one thing, the queen bee.

Meditation is relaxing and reposing in that atom. So, think of all the things that you could be grateful to, and ask what you want. And bless everybody. We receive, but not just receiving is enough, we should give and bless those who are in need.

We think Shiva is somewhere else sitting with a snake around his neck. Shiva is one in whom everything has taken birth, who encompasses everything right this moment, and in whom everything in creation dissolves. Every form you see in this creation is all his form.

There are three essential ingredients for the development of consciousness – Music, knowledge and silence. Knowledge is logical understanding. With a few moments of silence practised every day, we can shift our awareness. This is called Patrata. Building the capacity of the intellect can happen in a few moments of silence. This is all that is needed. The purpose of music is to lead to a space of silence and the purpose of knowledge is to lead to a space of wonderment.

What is happening right now? Sense of mindfulness, yes? I am not saying anything and you are waiting to catch something. Are you aware of this? Instead of catching something, put your attention into the waiting. This is mindfulness. It is meditative awareness. Are you getting what I am saying? What happens when you are mindful? Suddenly, a shift starts happening within you. From the scenery, you are going towards the seer. Now you are the seer and the scenery. You are looking at me, trying to understand what I am saying.

Take your attention back to yourself. You are sitting... reading...

Observe your breath. In your mind, understand something. All the time you are saying 'yes' or 'no' and having a private dialogue in your mind. It is like having a discourse with yourself. Are you getting what I am saying? The shift from scenery to the seer happens with yoga. It happens with Ujjai breath and meditation. It brings up an ocean of compassion within you. It makes the intellect sharp and attentive. You become more intuitive and aware. You become friendlier and more confident.

There are three levels of trust. First, when you have confidence in yourself, you are able to trust people around you. This is the trust in the goodness of people in society. There are so many good people here. Then, trust in something that is not seen but felt. It is too big to understand, yet cannot be dismissed. Lastly, there is trust in the divinity. Before your trust in God, you need to have trust in the goodness of the world. The world contains more good than what we think of. There are only a few confused, misguided and stressed out people who are involved in all sorts of violence. In general, the world is good.

□

Understanding the First Law of Spirituality

We often blame the world and this leads to blaming ourselves. The first law of spirituality is to stop blaming others as well as yourself. Have you taken this first step? Can you do that? Without this, there is no point in going ahead. Stop blaming others and yourself. Then see what happens. Such a burst of energy and enthusiasm comes up at once. I don't mean you should never find fault with yourself. Find mistakes in yourself and correct him/her. You must acknowledge your weaknesses and move on. This is different from blaming yourself. Have faith in yourself and in the goodness of society. Have faith in the essence of this whole creation.

Do you use cell phones? You need a SIM card for a cell phone to work. If you don't have a SIM card and you are dialling a number, you cannot reach anyone. Similarly, most of our prayers are not getting connected and that is why they are not being answered. My dear, you haven't put in the SIM card.

Now, you have put the SIM card but you are in the basement. Again, it doesn't work! You are not in range in the basement. It cannot pick up the signal. Similarly, you need a battery. You need a SIM card, a battery and range and only then you can call anyone, anywhere. In this way, our spirit needs to be calm, serene and settled. Knowledge, music and silence are the three things which make life complete. Prayers get answered. Keep singing with emotion. With faith, silence, confidence and knowledge, prayers get heard.

Stress can be eliminated through stress management, dispassion and through a broader outlook to life. When you are 90 years old

what do you want from this life? What do you want to take? What do you want to give? What impressions do you want to give to the world? What impressions do you want to take from the world? Just ponder. Just be with these few questions and the stress will leave you. Dispassion and breath uplift you. A little bit of devotion or bhakti uplifts you.

Sometimes I want to show anger and people don't believe me. That is my problem. Things work better with some anger. Anger is good if you are aware of it. It should last only as long as a line drawn on a water surface lasts. Some carry over anger from the previous day, previous month, or ten years ago. The mind suffers. Get out of anger, frustration, jealousy and greed. Meditation will help. Pranayama, Sudarshan Kriya and yoga are the answers.

Where does thought come from? It comes from a free mind or an un-free mind? Thoughts are not free. Free your mind of thoughts for a few moments. When astonished, shocked, in deep love, samadhi, meditation or deep sleep, your mind is free from thoughts. You get energized then.

We need to wake up to the power that we are made up of, that is love. Like our body is made up of amino acids, carbohydrates and protein, our spirit is made up of love. It is love that gets distorted and becomes all other negative emotions. It is wisdom which can keep love pure. Love without knowledge or wisdom is misery. Love plus wisdom is happiness. It is as simple as that.

What is this soul? We have heard so much about it, about self-realization. What is soul? What is self?

Want to know it? How many here have studied Physics or Chemistry? Everyone here must know a little about Physics. Our body is made up of billions of cells. Each cell in the body has a life. You use body scrub to get rid of dead skin cells. So many cells are

born and dying every day. You are not an individual person. This is how the ancient sages referred to it. You are a walking township. Purusha is a town. The soul lives in the town or the body that moves around. Do you know that in your intestines there are 50,000 bacteria?

This body is changing every day. Yet something is also not changing. To understand this, you should study a beehive. You must have seen a beehive. What keeps it there? The queen bee. Once the queen bee is gone, everything disappears. In the same way, your body is made up of billions of atoms. There is a queen bee in your body. Each body is a beehive full of honey. Locate the queen bee within yourself and that is meditation. Billions of atoms are present throughout your body. It is the same in a human body as in an ant or an elephant. The outer size of the body is irrelevant. It is the unknown or atma (self) which is non-changing. It always remains. Nothing can shake you with this knowledge. You will feel at home with everybody. Nothing will disturb you. This is the essence of spirituality.

God loves diversity. What if there is only okra to eat? But you have potatoes, tomatoes, beans, all kinds of fruit, vegetables and flowers. God seems to love diversity. He has created so many of us in different shapes, features and colours. He is definitely not a military person, an army general. A spirit that loves diversity must be diverse in itself too. That is what the rishis (ancient saints) found in meditation. There is only one Ganesh and one Vishnu, but in so many different forms. See unity in diversity and celebrate diversity. Our rishis in the past had spoken of tolerance, acceptance, diversity and equal opportunity.

Why is the difference? Find the common thread in different religions. According to different places, there are different customs. Time has created differences. There was one Buddha, now we have thirty-two forms of Buddhism, one Jesus Christ and now seventy-two sects of Christianity, and one Prophet Mohammed and now five different sects of Islam. In Hinduism, the variations cannot even be counted! But everyone believes in the Vedas, the Upanishads. How many different sects are there? Why should they not be there? Let it be there. See unity in diversity.

You forget the strength in you – Prayer and power of your sankalpa (positive intention). You keep doing practices and your things are taken care of. Don't ask for small things in your prayers. Ask for big things. Let government be good and stable, Let this knowledge reach out to many more people. It is up to you to make a divine society. You can start a collective movement. There are many good people and a very few people who cause disturbance, but their influence looks like they are many. You come together and you will find what difference you can make.

Recognizing your mistake and going forward is good. There is no point in hiding or justifying. Save the mind. When the mind is established, you can't do mistakes even if you want. With the knowledge of the self, all negative emotions like fear, anger and sorrow disappear.

Self is the ocean and the mind is a wave.

Clear your mind of all its negative impressions. When the mind is free from lust, greed, possessiveness, arrogance etc, when the mind is in the pure form with which we were all born then Nature listens to you. You are a child of nature and Nature loves you. When that manifests, when you are clear then two things happen – your wishes get fulfilled and you can fulfill others' wishes as well.

Misunderstandings happen on this planet because of distance, because there is no closeness, no one ever 'sits next to' the other. In one house, people live on different planets. In a town, people live in different galaxies.

Your body belongs to this society/ this world and the world/

society will take care of it. You belong to the Divine and the Divine will take care of you. In fact, the Divine is taking care of you. Make this distinction that you are separate from your body. As soon as you do this, you will see that you are separate from your body; you belong to the Divine. Your smile becomes a permanent feature.

Never link money with happiness. Even the poorest people are happy, if you see. In fact they are more happy. But money can create a false notion of security to you: You think if you have money, you have everything. The idea of money is for comfort, isn't it? Why do you want money? For comfort only but money can give you only one type of comfort – physical comfort. It doesn't give emotional and spiritual comfort.

If your partner is also on the path and understands you, it can enhance you both. If one is in doubt, the partner will help you to get over the doubt. If one is not doing the practice, the other one will pull him/her to do the practice and give him/her encouragement. Make him/her move on the spiritual path, so that much help comes from that. I have seen many couples – when one is going astray from the path, the other will pull him/her back onto the path. Because of the sake of the wife or husband, he/she continues being on the path, on the knowledge, on the spiritual path. This I have seen happening in many many families. Though, on the contrary, if both go in different directions and if one of him/her is not really on the path, it can be a hindrance for the other. It can be, though not necessarily.

Three things can help you to get over bad habits:

1. Love- If you love somebody or something, then promise him/her for their sake that you will continue the good habits.

2. Fear – When there is a fear that this bad habit is going to bring great problems to me, then you will get out of it.

3. Greed – If someone tells you that by giving up this bad habit,

you will get a million dollars, you would not do that (the bad habit), you want a million dollars in your pocket. If someone tells you, don't drink or smoke for the next one week, then you will be entitled to one million dollars. Will you smoke, will you drink? No ways! If someone tells you that you will get 10 million dollars or 10 million Euros if you don't smoke for one month or 30 days, you will say, 'Why only 30 days? I will not smoke for 35 days. I am sure of the number of days, as I want to be sure. Not 29 days. Some months are only 30, some are 31, so let me do for the maximum of 35 days.' Because you know, when you value something much more than the habit and you know that you are going to get that, then the habit will drop out of it. So through love, fear or greed you will stop doing it. You know, promiscuity has reduced to a great extent because of the fear of AIDS. After the dreadful disease of AIDS has started appearing, then promiscuity came down to a great extent. So similarly, commitment to a higher cause can help you get over small little attractions.

Love is a gift. If it is there, it is there, if it is not there, it is not there; you cannot force yourself to love somebody. Can you impose? If you do it, it will be contrary to what it is. You just be relaxed and go deep in the knowledge and suddenly one day, you will find that all are part of me and everybody is the same. Then love is not a verb, it's not an action. You don't have to love somebody, you are love, and you will understand that love is a noun. You are simply there as sparkling love. And that's it. Yes, obviously, it's not the give-and-take love of which you are talking about. You love somebody and they gave you something. Here people radiate that peace, so it is easy. They know all the basic course points of acceptance and not to be football and all these things. Definitely, it is much easier here and our job is to make the world like this so that anywhere in the world becomes much easier. All over the world, people say, 'Art of Living people have a smile on the faces'. There is a certain radiance, a certain confidence, a certain smile which is unparalleled. People comment on that all the time.

Listen to one thing now, you are right for the other person when you can adjust. Relationship means adjustment, it is giving. You give what you can to the other person and wait for him/her to give back to you. If you are demanding from the others, the relationship is not going to last long. Demand destroys the love. Demand and blame destroy relationships. So, you should only know how to praise others and uplift a situation instead of blaming, finding fault. Uplift the other, this should be your commitment. Then you are the right person for anybody, and everybody will love you when you don't hurt him intentionally. This is the first point. Number one. Second, you are open to correction and changes, you have the patience to listen to criticism. Three things, I am counting. You have patience to take in criticism. Fourth, you know the other persons' point of view, or where the shoe pinches, you know. You should see the other persons beyond their words and their actions. You know, when someone is working for 8 to 10 hours, when he comes back home, he is very tired. If he is a businessman and when the stock markets fall, he is so upset and he comes home to find solace. So you should see the circumstances, situations, how the spouse is and allow him the space to express his genuine feelings of frustrations, anger whatever.

You know, there is only one option when a person is angry or frustrated. The whole world expects him to keep the frustration to himselves, no one wants to share his frustration, but when he comes home, it is with his spouse. He explodes and expresses and shows all his frustration. At that time, the spouse should be there like a midwife – allow him to deliver. When someone is in labour pain, and if you say, 'Don't deliver, keep it, keep it, keep the baby inside.' What can she do? How long can you keep it inside? Somewhere you have to explode. When he comes with his stress, the spouse should allow him to express. Say, 'OK, download it. Download. Let go of all your stresses. OK whatever you want to blame, blame. You want to beat me or beat yourself, do it'. Then, you know, keep that type of space for him to un-stress and download. What you can say is 'Let go of all that you have carried all the day, all the stress of the

stock market or whatever else.' If a person commits a mistake at the workplace or injustice is done to him or her, he comes back and he wants some place to offload it. Offload is the right word I think, offload all that thing and one must keep that space for him to offload. Understand why he is upset, why he is unhappy – then your relationship will work. But you expect him not to tell anything, be nice to you all the 24 hours, 7 days a week and 365 days and find fault with him all the time.

Pricking him/her that 'you are useless, you are hopeless, you are this, that...' Poor lady or man! What will he/she do? He/she finds that he/she has no support. Nobody is helping him/her to grow, helping him/her, uplifting him/her and then he/she gets depressed. Right? So first, we will see. Greater is the person who has greater capacity to absorb, accommodate, adjust with anybody. If you can adjust with anybody, that much greater you are, you know and the degree can come less, less, less. If you know your acceptability is only 10 per cent, then you are thoroughly miserable if its zero per cent. There is no way you can grow in your life. Wisdom is to have this patience; grow from zero to one hundred per cent.

This is a good question – why am I here, what do I do? Keep asking. When you keep asking these questions, you either go crazy or become wise. I wish you became the latter, become much wiser, Ok? Don't tell me that crazy people are very wise. It's the other way round – wise people are sometimes crazy too.

Enjoy the world, without getting attached to it. You have to take a deep breath in. But you can't hold onto it. You have to let go (of the breath) to enjoy the fresh air. In life, it is the same thing. Letting go is important.

People who are free, regret that they don't have discipline. They keep promising that they will become disciplined.

People who are disciplined look for the end. Discipline is not

an end in itself, it is a means.

Look at the people who have no discipline; they are miserable. Freedom without discipline is absolute misery. Discipline without freedom is suffocating.

Orderliness is monotonous and chaos is stressful. We have to make the discipline free and the freedom disciplined.

People who are in company all the time, they look for the comforts of solitude. People who are in solitude, feel so lonely and want to be in company.

People who are in a cold place want to be in a warm place. People who are in a warm place love something cool.

This is the dilemma of life – Everyone is looking for perfect balance. Perfect balance is like a razor's edge. It can only be found in the self.

There is no road to this town and there are no steps to this house.

How do you get in? Figure it all out.

When you move with a connection to the divinity there is nothing that is richer than this. That rich feeling comes inside you when you feel connected to the divinity, connected to the infinite. When the wave remembers that it is connected to the ocean, that it is part of the ocean, that strength is enormous!

Every day you should meditate. You brush your teeth, you have a bath to keep your body clean. Similarly, you should listen to a little bit of knowledge and meditate. Cleansing of the intellect happens through knowledge – that knowledge which tells you that everything is impermanent. Music and harmony cleanses the emotions and enriches the heart. By giving, the heart becomes pure. With knowledge and meditation, everything becomes pure.

When someone dies, you realize that this is the truth. One day everyone is going to die. When you are alive you don't realize the truth. You are caught up in unwanted things.

Truth is something which you cannot avoid.

Beauty is something which cannot be renounced.

Love is something which cannot be expressed.

These three things are more than enough to remember. It is enough to digest.

You know why they say that marriages are made in heaven. It is because the choice is already made for you. You just have to take it and move on. You are free from choices. Move on with what you have on your plate.

You know the best thing is that you don't focus on the drawbacks. Focus on the positive. In a relationship if both the people have their focus on spirituality then they will move ahead together like parallel lines move, without clashing, to infinity. The moment they will shift their focus and focus on each other, there will be clashes. So it is very important that both are on the spiritual path.

First understand what freedom is. Drop whatever burden you feel in the mind. Quieten the mind. The mind will say: 'I want this', 'I want that' – drop everything. Have the sankalpa: I am happy, contented and don't need anything. When you are free, bliss follows you.

The Divine is not so sub-standard that you will 'have' to remember Him. Remembrance happens. Don't make an effort to remember. You have to remember something when it has not touched your heart. When the heart is kindled then you don't have to make an effort to remember that.

These are different names for the one Divinity. Like you wear a different dress every day. Today you are wearing black, tomorrow you will wear something else.

Even when you change your dress tomorrow, you will remain the same, right? The same way, whatever names and forms there are,

it is the same Divine.

Every human is pure but filled with dirt. Every human being is like a diamond. The fact that the diamond is in mud, does not make it mud. You simply have to pick it up and wash it. And it shines again. The shiny nature of a diamond is always there but covered with mud and slush.

When you are in action, don't get into this philosophy of doership or non-doership, else the mind gets confused. When you act, you act a hundred per cent. When you are acting a hundred per cent, suddenly you will realize I am not doing, it is all happening. Non-doership is an experience; it is not something you try to do or achieve.

Our breath is linked to our emotions. For every emotion, there is a particular rhythm in the breath. So, when you cannot directly harness your emotions, with the help of breath you can do that. If you are in theatre, you would know that a director asks you to breathe faster when you have to show anger. If you have to show a serene scene, the director would tell you to breathe softer and slower.

If we understand the rhythm of our breath, we are able to have a say over our mind, we can win over any negative emotions like anger, jealousy, greed, and we are able to smile more from our heart. I think we need to bring the child-like beauty and innocence, that God gifted every human being, back into our lives.

Understanding Children

We all are children in some sense. I wish we were more of a child than an adult. You know, a child smiles 400 times a day, an adolescent smile 17 times and an adult does not smile at all. There will be very less conflicts in the world if people in the world can only smile more.

Unfortunately, today, the pride is associated with aggression and violence. Someone who is aggressive and loses temper easily is considered heroic in schools and colleges. We need to make the shift

from attaching pride to violence to attaching pride to non-violence. We need to give our children a world vision of violence-free and stress-free society.

I am sure we can achieve this by five things in our hands:

1. The first thing is music and dance.

2. The second is – sports. With the advent of computer and video games, children don't go out and play as they used to do before. They lock him/herselves up with video games, most of which are violent. We need to give an orientation to function more in sports.

3. The third is travel. We conduct programmes in India, America, sometimes in Europe, Poland, Germany, also here in black forest, where we bring children from all countries together for a week. Many times, they speak their own languages, but just being with one another creates such a bonding between him/her that the barriers melt down and they feel at home.

We should help him/her travel around and communicate with the people of other cultures and religions.

We need to give children multi-cultural and multi-religious education. I feel all the children should know a little bit about all the knowledge in the world – Hinduism, Buddhism, Judaism, Christianity, Catholicism, Shaoism, Shintoism. A little bit understanding of all the major religions and cultures of the world helps them grow up with a broad mindset. Even if a small part in the world is left with people thinking that only they are right, the world will not be a safe place to live. The sense of belongingness, that we belong to one global family in spite of different colours, languages and food habits, has to be developed in children and youths.

4. The fourth thing is involving kids in some service projects. There is such an opening that happens in youths when they are associated with some service project.

5. Then is Yoga and meditation. I have made yoga so secular that people from any religious background have no objection in doing it. It is just some breathing techniques and some postures, not attached to any belief system.

Violence does not mean self-protection nor does non-violence mean lack of self-defense. You should be prepared for your self-defense no doubt, but in your mind and heart you nurture non-violence. And you will see in the presence of non-violence, such strong non-violence, even violent people will drop their violent tendencies.

It has happened several times with me, when I was in Washington DC, another time in Los Angeles. On both occasions, a gentleman wanted to attack me. He cursed me in the name of Jesus and said that this was all satanic; Yoga was satanic. As soon as he came, this tall hefty guy, I said, 'Wait.' We didn't have any weapons and we didn't have any defence. He just went down on his knees and started crying. Everybody was so surprised, it was a satsang, like this, nobody expected a man to attack.

I just said, 'Wait, wait,' and he bowed down and started crying. Later on, he took the course.

You know, it is a misconception that could cause violence. It is stress and a sort of victimization that could cause violence. But when we believe in non-violence and we walk with that power in our hearts you will find a big change. There are so many such events.

A long time ago, I was in Delhi and Noida. Thousands of people came with torches to burn my car. I just showed my hand and said, 'Wait; okay, you can do whatever you want. I just want ten minutes to talk to you. But that's it; in those ten minutes they all changed. In those days, in 1980, Noida was not developed, it was all a jungle, a village with dacoits. So we must believe in non-violence and I don't mean you should not carry a weapon or learn self-defence.

Negative people bring out lots of skills in you. You should thank him/her, they teach you how to deal with him/her, how to man oeuvre through all those situations. They make you move ahead. And they push all the buttons and make you free from buttons.

If someone is a compulsive liar, what to do?

Somebody asked me a question yesterday, 'Guruji, are you angry with me?' I said, 'No.' That does not mean you can go on lying. Now, I know some people do wrong things, say wrong things and misuse the trust of other people. They say, 'I have just spoken to Guruji on the phone and he has said like this.'

I forgive and I don't get angry but I feel compassion for him/her because they are putting mud on their own heads. They are causing trouble for him/herselves. So why should I spoil my mind getting angry with such people? I don't feel angry but feel compassion that they go and create trouble here and there.

Pitaji had written a quote, 'The world is full of people and mistakes. Forgive the mistakes and love the people.' What a wonderful thing he has said!

If someone has done something wrong to you, see it from this angle that the person was just a postman to do what he did. Yes, this is number one. The second angle is, the person was ignorant he didn't know what he was doing that is why he was doing it, right. The third is to see that person is a victim himself/herself, so he did the mistake the way he did it. In this way you broaden your vision. Suddenly you will see things are all turning around.

When Lord Krishna sat in Samadhi, that is, when he recited the Gita. After the war, once Arjuna asks him, 'I have forgotten the beautiful knowledge that you gave me. At that time there was a lot of crowd and so much commotion on the war field and I didn't listen to you properly. Please tell me again what you said.' Then Krishna replied, 'No, I can't tell you now. At that time I was in samadhi, so I made you sit and whatever came to me I told you at that time; now I cannot tell you again.'

So, whatever Lord Krishna said was not a person saying this knowledge, but the universe speaking. These messages came from

the Shiva tattva, the atma tattva.

He said, 'I am the sun, I am the rain, truth and untruth, everything is me.' This is very deep knowledge.

If you see everything is made from one tattva, from atoms. What is your mother made of, father made of? Everyone's body is made from the same thing, from foodgrains. Foodgrains are consumed and the body is developed, whoever eats, they all grow and the body is made from that. So everyone is made from one substance, one power and one energy. So, he is saying the whole world is made from that one consciousness, one energy, one substance.

Now if you see the fan, mike and light are all working with one current, with electricity, isn't it? But it seems like the mike is different, the light is different and the fan is something else. They all look different, but they are all made up of the same thing. In the same way, if the sun was not there, then the earth cannot exist. If the earth was not there, how could there be plants or trees or human beings? So what is our source? First from the physical aspect, our source is the earth; more subtle than that it is the sun. What is the source of the sun? The universal energy – and so Lord Krishna says that universal energy is ME.

That is the atma that is you and that is me and everything is made of this universal energy and this is what today's scientist also say. Those who study quantum physics, this is what they say – that the whole world is made up of one energy. Earlier it was said that there were different protons and electrons functioning and making things work, but now they say it is all one energy, everything is a wave function. What we consider physical things are not there in reality, it is all just energy and this is what Lord Krishna has said many years ago in the Bhagavad Gita.

'Avajananti mam mudham manusim tanumasritam, Param bhavam ajananto mama bhuta- mahesvaram', these people do not see my true nature as that one universal Energy, consciousness and they are thinking I am a human being. I am in a human body but the consciousness inside me is that Supreme Consciousness. I am not a human being. I am a power.

It is said in Vishnu Sahasranamam 'Sohamékena shlokena stuta evana sumshayaha', in one Soham everything has come. One thousand names of Vishnu are written in one word 'Ram' and that is also written in 'Soham'. Sometimes you can put on Vishnu Sahasranamam, listen to it and meditate, that is fine. All mantras have an effect but the most important is meditation. Going beyond the mantras is also necessary, letting go of that as well, your mind remains calm and peaceful.

Being silent and knowing that the divinity is taking care of everything – that is the best form of prayer; the best prayer is meditation.

Break through all barriers and feel that you are blessed; this is the one and the only step you have to take. The rest will all happen.

If you're not feeling close to the Guru, it's because of you. Because of your mind, because of your ego concepts. Share with the Guru that which is very important or intimate to you. Share that. Do not feel shame, shy or judgmental about yourself.

Unless you express to the Master that which is very intimate and important to you, just being on the formal and informal communication levels cannot make you feel close. 'How are you, where are you going? How have you been?' Stop formal and superficial conversations with the Master and speak with your heart that which is very important and intimate, very deep to your life. Don't just say – how much does the squash costs, 30 cents or whatever?

If you don't feel close to the Master, there's no point in having a Master. It is just another burden to you. You have enough already. Just say, 'Goodbye,' get rid of it.

You should feel more close if you are pushed away, scolded or

ignored. In order to ignore somebody takes a lot of effort. When a Master does not even ignore wrapping paper, or a flower that is in a vase, how can he ignore a walking, talking, breathing human being who is connected? How could that be ignored? So when you understand this, you already feel close.

Effort and surrender go hand in hand. So put your effort and surrender. That is why we take a sankalpa and then leave it. In pooja, what do we do? We take rice, water, flowers in our hand and take a sankalpa then we don't hold on to the flowers. We drop them. When you go to the cinema, you first buy a ticket and then you give the ticket back when you are going inside the hall. You have to give it, right? 30 to 40 years ago you had to give the ticket, now also you have to give it, right? So, in this way, we must take a sankalpa and then surrender. We give our 100 per cent and then leave it to God's will.

You assume that you have devotion. Don't strive to have devotion. We should assume that we have love and devotion in us. When you believe in this, the devotion in you enhances. When you think you don't have devotion at all, it wouldn't manifest.

□

Understanding the Essence of the Bhagwad Gita

When Ashtavakra imparted the knowledge to King Janaka, wonder arose in him. 'Ah'! King Janaka wondered, 'How did I not recognize this truth for so long!'

Once he realized this truth, he said, 'Salutations to myself!' Namo mahyam! The transforming experience that 'I am the paramatma, the Divine consciousness' came to him.

The knowledge dawned that there is no difference between myself and the Divine consciousness which is omnipotent, omnipresent and omniscient.

Leaving behind the limited mind and being established in the infinite consciousness is the Ashtavakra Gita.

We search for the Divine everywhere except within us. The process of worship is to lead us from the external world to within. The highest expression of pooja is meditation. In pooja, we use and honour the five elements which form the basis of this creation and we honour ourselves as well.

When we do achamanam (offering of oblations), we offer water to Kesava, the Divine within us. Each process in the pooja leads us within.

When you go to sleep at night, think that the Divine is within me, 'Salutations to the Divine in my heart!' Meditate upon this, and then go to sleep. Then see how the quality of your sleep is!

There is no difference between the Guru, the Self and the Divine. Antarmukhi sada sukhi – He who perceives the Divinity within, whose mind is turned inward, is always happy.

The Divine consciousness is not limited like the body but is

present everywhere like space.

Honouring this divine consciousness is the Ashtavakra Gita.

When you are in front of television, do you listen to the voice first or watch the screen? They happen simultaneously, isn't it? In the same way, both karma (action) and bhagya (good fortune) are important. When we perform appropriate actions, then we become bhagya, or fortunate. When we have good fortune, then our actions are fruitful.

I have no troubles. That is why I can take away yours. If the doctor is sick, then can he heal you? Since I have no problems, you have come to me.

Understanding the Nirvana

You know our senses always look outward and the mind through the senses always captures the world around us and then whatever the senses capture is stored inside. You look at a scenery and the scenery gets imprinted in your mind. You taste coffee and the taste and flavour, fragrance of coffee, everything gets imprinted in your consciousness. You taste apple pie or chocolate and that gets imprinted in your mind. Similarly with sound and touch; you touch a certain part of the body and that creates a sensation and the mind starts craving for those sensations. So these impressions in the mind are like a screen between you and the world outside.

Now the more the impression the more it is stifling for the life-force or life-energy, the prana. Just imagine you go and sit and watch a movie in the morning, afternoon, evening; do it for three days and see what happens. You brain loses balance; you go haywire. So many impressions, three movies a day and for three days, that's it, you are ready to get into mental hospital. Then on the fourth day if you are asked to watch a movie you will say, 'Oh no, please I want to shut my eyes.' The ability of the senses to enjoy is limited but the hunger of the mind could be unlimited, you know. Bulimia is one such solid example. Your stomach says, 'Please no, but your heart says, No, I want more' so, you stuff in more when there is no place and then you throw out and then again eat. So it is an imbalance between the capacity/ability to enjoy and the desire to enjoy.

Nirvana is bringing the balance and having no desire. You know desire means a lack, desire indicates lack. If it is all there then why would you desire? You desire a car because it is not there right now with you. You desire something that which you don't have. When

your consciousness is fulfilled, it says I want nothing, I am satisfied, I am fulfilled; that is Nirvana. Even hankering for enlightenment is an obstruction for enlightenment.

There is the story of Lord Buddha. Lord Buddha was in search of knowledge. He did everything that everybody said. Someone said, 'You do this japa' He did that; someone else said, 'You fast,' and he did that. He fasted and fasted because at that time there was another enlightened person called Mahavir who had attained enlightenment and who never ate food, so the whole Jain tradition started with control on food where they ate every other day or didn't eat because the propounder, the prophet of the Jain philosophy, Mahavir ate very little food. In several days, he ate just once because he was in bliss that He didn't need it.

So the Buddha tried to copy this by also fasting in the hope that by fasting He might get enlightened but then He became so weak that He could not even walk. He barely pulled himself and sat under a tree and almost collapsed when someone came and brought Him a bowl of milk pudding and He drank that and broke all the vows of fasting and had a good sleep that night. The morning when He woke up there was nothing left; the last star was going down the horizon, the dawn was coming up and something happened within Him. Suddenly, He realized that's it, there is nothing to look for now. He had been looking for joy here and there but now there is nothing to look for anywhere and He just sat that moment, that freedom dawned on Him. That freedom is called Nirvana, freedom from everything.

See in life from childhood we keep hanging on to something or another, as a child you are hanging on to little toffees and toys and then you grow a little older it is toys and friends and then you grow a little older and you are hanging on to friends and a little older then children, grandchildren. Something or another kept occupying your mind, you got lost in outer relationships. My son, my daughter-in-law, my grand children, my this, my that and it took your whole life, your whole day, your whole time or you started caring for this or that, you are worried for the world, so something or another occupied your mind. So, your mind could never reflect on who I am; what I am; what I want, what life is.

It never had time, even all the religious prayers we did were for the welfare of something, to get something. You sat and prayed, 'Oh' let my son be okay; my daughter be okay, let my life be comfortable; let me have money; let me have fame; let me have something. You thank God for giving you this or that. Our prayers are all geared for getting something or thanking for what we have already got. That means we are still latching on to objects, people and relationships.

Nirvana is that freedom, when mind is free it says I want nothing I have everything. I have everything this is all mine, anyway I have no need for anything. That state is called Nirvana and the same is called Samadhi, you know Nirvana or Moksha in Sanskrit. Moksha means freedom, liberation, mind free from all the hang-ups.

Suppose you are taken from here and put on Mars, another planet where you know nobody and you have nobody, how would you feel? Just imagine, you are taken and thrown in a distant planet. There is nobody around, what happens? You go blank, there is nothing! All our emotions are linked with people, objects, and concepts. When you get freedom from the impressions of people, impressions of different events, emotions, objects and when your mind is free from all concepts and even the concept of Nirvana. Last obstruction is hankering for Nirvana, I want to be free, I want to be free. This wanting to be free can also be bondage. That state of nothingness is Nirvana.

In simple terms, it is said freedom from sorrow. Sorrow is because of the sense of mine. Someone loses his purse or cell phone, you don't get affected but when you lose your own cell phone or your purse, you get affected. What is the difference? There is a story, a father gave his home in the valley to his son and asked him to take care of the home and the father left for a long pilgrimage, trekking in the mountains. After a month or so when he came back, he saw his house in the Kashmir valley burnt down. The house was not there; it was burnt down into ashes and the father became miserable and started crying, 'Oh my God! everything is gone, everything!' By the time his son returned from the field. He saw the father beating his chest and yelling, crying and howling. He said, 'Dad, what happened?'

'What happened? See my life-savings, everything is gone,

everything is finished, my home is burnt down.' The son said, 'Dad, I already sold the house and I got double the money. A very good offer came, so I immediately sold it. Someone came from another town and they were willing to pay double the money and they wanted the home, so I sold the home, dad.'

Suddenly, the tears immediately changed and a smile came on the father's face. The situation was the same; it was his house. First he felt it was my house burnt down; now it was somebody else's house and then he said, 'Anyway, it was an old house. It burnt down; maybe it was purposefully burnt down; now we can build a nice new bungalow.' He started talking the other way around. It is mine, because of that I get more pain.

Me is lost in mine. Nirvana is getting back to me from mine. Instead of mine, mine, you go back to me, who I am; and when the Buddha went to find who He was He found nothing. He said I could not find an atma, I could not find a soul. It is all nothing, there is no self, no soul, there is nothing but the one who is experiencing this nothing is me. I experience nothing, I experience Moksha. Who should the nirvana happen to, It's me. It is not the ego me but the 'me' as a consciousness which is ease-ness, which is everywhere. So the 'me' is not an individual person but 'me' is a field of consciousness. This is exactly what the Vedanta says, 'Atma is not an entity; it is a field. The being without impression is mukti, liberation.'

To say it very simply, from mine to the 'me' that is lost in mine and because of that it is miserable. The seer is lost in the scenery. Everything is scenery including our body. The mind derives from the scenery to the seer. First, it gets onto the body and becomes aware of the body, then behind the body there is the mind, behind the mind is the intellect and then the ego; pass one layer after another and go deep. It is like the peeling of an onion, you know. An onion has many sheets, Nirvana is like peeling the onion, not this, not that, going deep inside to the centre core. What do you find in the centre core of an onion? Nothing!

Now what is the use of finding this, the mind asks. Freedom from sorrow, freedom from misery, FREEDOM!

Lord Buddha said only four things, the first things he said is,

there is sorrow, don't deny it. Life is miserable; married people are miserable, unmarried people are miserable. People with children are miserable and people without children are miserable. Life is sorrow, people who have fame are miserable and people who are hankering for fame are miserable. People who have power and position are miserable and those who do not have are also miserable. People who have money are more miserable than those who do not have. There is misery everywhere. You have friends and you are miserable or you don't have friends and you are miserable. When you don't have any friends at least you are miserable in a different manner, you are miserable because you don't have something but when you have friends and you consider your friends as the cause of your misery, this is even worse. So there is misery and there is a cause for misery. No one is miserable for no reason; there is a reason to be miserable. If you are sad you cannot be sad for no reason, your sadness is connected to something, so there is a cause for misery; the second principle of Lord Buddha. The third principle He said is, there is a way and it is possible to eliminate misery. It is possible because it is not your nature, like you cannot eliminate sweetness from sugar because sweetness is the nature of sugar. You cannot eliminate heat from fire because the nature of fire is heat. If it is your nature there is no way you can eliminate it but it is possible to eliminate misery and there is a method for it, a way for it. So what is it? The cause of misery is the seer got stuck in the scenery. You know if you see innocent villagers they go to a movie and if the hero is crying they cry; innocent people, they don't realize it is only in the movie that the villain is getting victorious. People get so angry and they throw tomatoes and stones on the screen, at least in the past they used to do that. Even in the plays, people got so engrossed in it that they would throw things on the screen. The seer got engrossed in the scenery; this is the cause of misery and it is possible for the seer to retrieve back. However miserable you are, you cannot be miserable for 24 hours. You take some rest, you sleep and your mind gets back from the scenery. However beautiful or ugly, pleasurable or painful the seer cannot be with the scenery all the time. In sleep you retrieve and the mind comes back to the seer but consciously

when the mind leaves the scenery and gets back to the seer and sees that this is all temporary, everything is changing, everything!

Including our own body everything is impermanent and when this becomes very clear that everything is impermanent, all relationships are impermanent, people are impermanent, our body is impermanent, our feelings are impermanent, suddenly the consciousness or the mind which was logging onto things becoming miserable turns back onto oneself. Me, I am… that return from mine to 'me', from the scenery to the seer is the method. From the scenery get back to the seer and reposing in the seer is Nirvana. You are reposing, content, and you find that the seer is all bliss, all love, all that we have been seeking outside in many things are all what the seer is.

It is said that the Buddha didn't utter a word for seven days after He had total contentment, the experience of Nirvana, he didn't say a word. He just moved several steps up and down and it is said that the angels came and prayed to Him to speak; if you don't speak what will happen, you should speak. Then the Buddha said, 'People who know they know it and people who don't know they don't know by speaking it is not going to help.' Then the angels persuaded Him, 'there are some people who are on the border line and if You speak to him/her they will immediately catch it and it will help him/her. You should speak.' It is then said that the Buddha started speaking. Brahma, the creator came and told Him you should speak. You know there are a lot of stories to that effect.

The main idea is freedom from misery, that is Nirvana; totally free from desires; freedom from misery, freedom from pleasures and hankering for pleasure. You see it is the hankering for pleasure which causes misery and not knowing this is all ephemeral, everything is dissolving, disappearing, everything is changing causes sorrow. However nice something is, however ugly something is, both will disappear into thin air. Knowing this you get back to the self.

When we eat our food every day, we must remember with gratitude the farmer who has worked for it. Anna Dhata Sukhi Bhava

is a traditional blessing that wishes happiness to the giver of food. We should bless the soldiers who guard our borders at the cost of their own lives. They are the wealth of our nation. They should be happy and their families should be happy. Our blessings will surely reach them.

Meditate! Sit quietly and meditate, or listen to some chanting music. All this will help. Meditation, some pranayama, Sudarshan Kriya, some exercises, ujjayi breath are very good for fears. Don't think that fear is somewhere deep inside you. It is an erroneous notion of psychology that fear and guilt are deep down. I tell you, deep down there is only a lot of joy; a lot of bliss. And in that centre – no fear, no guilt, no anger, no lust can touch you. Deep down you are wonderful. So never think you have all these anxieties. Those who say that there is something wrong deep down are blind. It is all there just on the surface. If they call that deep then I will suggest to go deeper. In the centre of your being, you are a fountain of joy. Saying, 'Oh! My Mind! Deep down there is anxiety!' is ignorance; a wrong idea and concept. The moment you accept these words as truth, it starts becoming more difficult to get over those emotions. They become more permanent there.

The world is full of people and mistakes. Forgive the mistakes and love the people.

Wherever you are, you meditate and you find the divinity.

It is okay that you don't go to temple after temple. Wherever you are, you meditate and you find the divinity. The Divine is everywhere. You don't have to run to temples. That is the first stage; you have crossed that stage and have come to the second stage where Hari comes to you. There is a saying that when Kabir was calling, 'Hari, Hari, Hari' he didn't find Hari. But when he started meditating, he said, 'Ab Hari lage peeche keheth Kabir, Kabir', Hari is now coming

to me wherever I am.

If you are an astrologer know that the work of an astrologer is very good. You can give people some direction, this will be beneficial. Sometimes people have Ashtama Guru, Ashtama Shani. Make him/her aware that they have Ashtama Guru, and they need to be a little careful. Those who have Ashtama Shani, this brings trouble to the mind. So advise people to be cautious.

Like this, give advice to people. You must do that. That is how people will understand why sometimes too many thoughts arise in the mind, or so many doubts come and one does not have any interest in doing anything. Then when an astrologer explains that this is the reason why the mind is disturbed and it will get okay and these are the remedies; it will help. Everyone should chant 'Om Namah Shivaya', all the negative effects due to planetary positions will be neutralized with the chanting of 'Om Namah Shivaya'. Negative effects become very less, as good as gone.

That is why one field of astrology is remedies. There is a saying that an arrow was coming which was supposed to hit the head, just blew a few strands of hair and went away.

Every person has emotions. Who is not emotional? Everybody has some emotions. But if you label yourself as emotional by nature then you are giving a license to yourself not to be intelligent or you are giving a license to yourself to be weak. You can be emotional but you can't be emotionally weak. Wake up and see you are not weak, you are strong. You have to assume you are strong.

You must have heard the story of Mullah Nasiruddin. Mullah Nasiruddin started thinking that he was dead. So walking here and there he kept saying, 'I am a dead body; I am dead.' If someone would ask him something he would say, 'A dead body cannot talk; I am a dead body,' even though he was speaking. So his wife got very concerned, anything she would ask him he would say, 'I am a dead body; why are you asking me?' So she took him to a psychologist, and the psychologist told him, 'Look you are not dead; you are alive,' but he said, 'No, I am a dead body.' So the psychologist told him, 'In a dead body there is no blood; there is water,' and he agreed. So the psychologist took a needle and pricked him and he started to bleed. Then the psychologist said; 'See that means you are not a dead body; you are alive.' Then Mullah says, 'Today I have found out that there is blood even in dead bodies.'

So in this way whatever we believe ourselves to be, we become that. So we should not think 'I am emotionally weak.' Who said you are emotionally weak? Wake up now and see that you are strong. Emotions are natural and it is very beautiful to have emotions. Otherwise, you will become so dry. Even the elephant here has emotions. Birds, elephants, horses, cows and buffaloes, they all have emotions, even a dog has emotions. Then how can you not have emotions? There are emotions in you as well, but to think I am emotional, I am weak, this label which you have put on yourself needs to be taken off. You are fine with the emotions; there is no need to beat yourself up. You need to feel from inside that I am strong. If tears come sometimes, there is nothing wrong in that. But don't get too carried away with your emotions.

Just reading a menu card your stomach does not get full. If fire is written on paper it does not burn your hands. The difference between fire written on paper and fire in reality, this is the difference. You have intellectually understood that enlightenment is here and now; but to experience it, it happens only in meditation. The techniques take the mind away from the cravings, aversions and all the obstructions that have come to be here and now.

Bliss comes out of chaos and the ability to enjoy chaos is enlightenment.

The anger of a wise man does so much good, and the love of an ignorant person causes more problems. See, an illiterate mother, an uneducated mother, she doesn't like her children going to school

because the young ones cry while going to school. Then she says, 'No, no. OK, don't go to school.' They say they don't want to study, and she says, 'OK, don't study.' Her love for her children has spoiled their whole life, isn't it? So, even the love of an ignorant person does harm. And even the anger of a saint always does good.

There are so many stories about one sage; his name was Durvasa. In India, if someone is very angry, they say, 'Oh, he is a Durvasa!' means he is someone who gets angry at the drop of a hat. But he would come back to normal state immediately. This is to say; don't feel bad about yourself if you have anger.

Even a Rishi had some anger. So, you don't have to be too hard on yourself by blaming yourself. That is just to give you self-confidence. To make you feel, you are OK, in spite of your little bit anger. That is only one rare case. That is to say that enlightenment is unconditional. Then what is it? It is unconditional. You can't put any condition on that freedom. Just to tell you, there is no condition. So it's possible to get angry as well. And, sometimes anger can also do good.

Imagine a movie with no villain. Imagine there is only a hero who is eating, sleeping and generally just hanging around with nothing to do! Would you watch such a movie? Opposite values are complementary. Both thorns and petals exist. You have the choice to pick up either the thorns or the petals. God is there within. He is sometimes sleeping and hiding, sometimes awake and dancing. After some sadhana, God is awake. Then He is rocking. Awaken the god and the goddess in you! A stone does not feel, but a living being does. Waking the godliness in you is essential. This is why there are particular hymns sung in India in the morning, 'Wake up and bless us, O Lord!' On one level, it sounds ridiculous. It is the parents' job to wake up children, but in this hymn, human beings are singing to the gods to wake up and bless the creation. This is a paradox, and in this paradox, is hidden a deep secret of existence.

Attachment brings pain, but nothing comes without pain. We came into this world in a lot of pain. The process of birth itself is very painful. For nine months, we were comfortable and then suddenly the ocean around us disappeared and we had to come out! Attachment happens when your focus is not on the Being, but on the outside. Wanting to control, possess and hold on brings pain. When we are relaxed and content, love transforms to bliss. Demand and control only bring pain. Wisdom, along with love, is the answer.

Anger comes out of your love for perfection. Create some space for imperfection around you. Make a list of all the things you consider to be wrong. Then have people around you do everything on that list! When you get angry, just observe that sensation. Observe how your teeth are clenching and how the mind becomes. Take a few long deep breaths and see if it changes. However, I have no experience, since I myself have never had this problem. So my advice may not be authentic. You should ask others. There are many here who will tell you. After the regular practice of Sudarshan Kriya, anger tends to settle down.

Imagine we live for eighty years. Out of that, twenty-five or thirty years we simply sleep. Ten years we spend in the bathroom. Another ten years, we are stuck in traffic. Then so many years we spend being sad and miserable. Ultimately, only some two or three years we spend in prayer, service and so on.

Music unites us and meditation takes us very deep. It brings integrity in us. If you see the Indian goddess of Learning (Saraswati), she sits on a rock. The rock is stable. It symbolizes that knowledge once learnt, neither moves nor leaves. Whereas the goddess of Wealth (Lakshmi) sits on a lotus flower. The rain comes and the flower sways with the flow of water. The goddess of Learning sits on a rock. She has an instrument, a book and a rosary in her hands. The book

symbolizes knowledge, the instrument symbolizes music and the rosary symbolizes meditation. These three aspects – wisdom, knowledge and music – must be brought into our life.

When you say a word, you have already heard a definition for it. I would say enlightenment is a connection with the Universal Spirit, realizing that you are part of it, you are that. Giving unconditional love without any effort, you don't have to put any effort for that. Being like an open book, being natural and all these qualities are there in every individual. It only needs a little nurturing and then it starts blossoming. So when you walk, walk like you are enlightened, you are open, you are like a child, and you are free – emotionally, mentally and intellectually. Enjoy the freedom. When you don't have any cravings and aversions of your own then you can give yourself a certificate that you are enlightened. But you should be over all your cravings and aversions. Clear heart, clear mind and clarity in action are all part of enlightenment. If you look at a child of two-three years, or a baby of six months – there is an unconditional love in his/her eyes. Every baby has all these qualities, but minus wisdom. When you grow old keep all these qualities in you like innocence, and have the depth of wisdom along with it. That is what it is.

A Guru only wants the disciple to progress, to blossom, not to be unstable, just be happy, unselfish and serve people. And whatever a disciple wants from the Guru, the Guru keeps on bestowing that. Initially, a disciple asks for little things and then asks for great things. The Guru sometimes gives him the little things he wants and sometimes doesn't.

Your body belongs to this world and the world will take care of it. You belong to the Divine and the Divine will take care of you.

When these eyes meet yours, will you not catch a glimpse of love?
Take just one step forward, will you not find the entire way?

Extend your hand, will you not find the work is done?

Smile just once; will the world not make you its own?

Take the name even once; will your life not be fulfilled?

Anything which enhances the spirit is spirituality.

Anything that brings energy in you is spirituality.

Anything that makes you intelligent is spirituality.

Anything that uplifts lifeforce in you is spirituality.

Anything that brings care and compassion is spirituality.

Anything that connects you with the Universal Spirit is spirituality.

Life is a journey where you turn a question into a wonder.

10,000 years ago, a little boy of 8-9 years asked his father about God.

The boy to his father: What is God and how does God Look?

His father takes him by the hand and brings him out of his house. He asked him, 'What was there at the place of their house before it was built?'

The boy said, 'Space.'

Father: Where is the house built?

Boy: Space.

Father: What will exist and what will remain when this house will demolish?

Boy: Space.

Father: That is God.

God is not a person sitting somewhere. It is so depicted in paintings only. God is love, God is the space in which everything exists, from which everything has come into existence, and in which everything dissolves. God is the space, joy and love, which is all pervading. The space around you is not the dead space. It is filled

with energy and intelligence. That energy and intelligence is divinity. It is everywhere – your inside as well as your outside.

Most of the native cultures of the world have the same concept. They say God is in the mountains, in the rivers, in the flowers, in the trees, in the animals, and in the human beings. God is love. You can feel it but cannot see it. You can experience that enormous energy when you go deep in meditation.

Complaints are opinions. Listen to him/her carefully, and if there is something good in them then you can take that. If it is just a biased opinion, smile at is. That's my policy. You can take something on board. I suggest you should take criticism with an open mind, and also give criticism with an open mind. You should never be shy about criticism.

What is great is, when you can smile at complaints. That means you have achieved something.

Wealth is the means, but if it becomes a goal in itself, then it leads to insecurity.

Personality is the one that people perceive. The whole journey of life is from being somebody to becoming nobody, and from being nobody to be a part of everybody. If someone is stuck with the idea of personality, there is less scope for him/her to grow.

Everything is changing. People change; their ideas change. Let us acknowledge this basic fact. So, if you have judged then even your judgment can change.

Management is all about just going along with what exists. Not making something new, but going along with what is there already.

There are 7 points that India can be proud of and that have not been explored yet.

Food: There are so many varieties of food in India. Tripura, a small place in India, has more than 200 varieties of food. North Indians don't know the different kinds of South Indian dishes. Even South Indians don't know the dishes from North India. We don't market ourselves properly. We have the greatest varieties possible in the world, yet we don't project ourselves.

Tourism: We have a great part of history which we don't capitalize.

Music and Dance: There are so many types of dance and music which we haven't even projected so far.

Dress and Jewellery: The Indian dress is appreciated the world over. We have no pride of what we wear. Places like Thailand and Indonesia are very proud of their dresses and jewellery. We are not. We don't feel good about ourselves. Low self-esteem is eating our attitude and culture.

Information Technology: This will take India to new heights.

Ayurveda: There are 280 kinds of flora and fauna available in India which is not available anywhere in the world. We don't pay any attention to that. These are going to be the future medicine of the 21st century.

Triphala: Foreigners have taken this formula and patented it. Similarly, things are happening all over the world.

Indian Spiritual Values: The yoga market is valued at $27 billion in the United States itself. 99% of local US people dominate this market. They started preparing materials for yoga which is a product of India and our gift to the world. People are invited to do mantras and chanting in some building in New York. All across India, in temples, if someone is chanting, we don't even bother to look at him/her.

□

Glossary

Aarti: A Hindu ritual of worship in which light from wicks soaked in ghee (purified butter), or camphor is offered to one or more deities

Aashadha: The 4th month of the Hindu Calendar

Adharma: irreligiosity; unrighteousness; sin

Advaita: Non-Duality

Asana: Yoga posture

Ashtama Guru: Jupiter in the 8th house of the Hindu horoscope

Ashtama Shani: Saturn in the 8th house of the Hindu horoscope

Atma: Soul

Ayurveda: The ancient Hindu science of health and medicine

Bhajan: Songs of Devotion

Bhakti: Devotion

Brahmagyaan: Knowledge of God

Deva: god

Devta: god

Dharma: Obligations and duties and regulations over actions, words and behaviour.

Dhyan: Contemplation

Diksha: Initiating a disciple with transcendental knowledge or mantra by which he/she becomes freed from all forms of materialism

Dwaita: Duality

Guna: Quality; the three modes of nature: sattva, rajas, tamas

Gyan: Knowledge

Gyani: The one who is knowledgeable

Idli: A south Indian rice cake

Jyeshtha: The third month of the Hindu Calendar

Jyotish Shastra: Astrology

Kaliyuga: The fourth (present) age of the world, characterized by total decadence

Kirtan: A Hindu devotional song in which lines are sung by a leader and then repeated by a larger group

Kripa: Grace

Kriya: Action that purifies one leading into deeper spirituality, towards self-realisation

Laya: Rhythm

Mangalsutra: A necklace worn by a woman after her marriage. It is one of the symbols of being a married woman

Moksha: Nirvana; liberation of the soul from the cycle of birth and death; enlightenment

Parmatma: Supreme God

Pooja: Worship; adoration

Poornima: Full Moon

Prana: life-force; life-energy; breath of life

Pranayama: Extension of the prana or breath

Rajasic / Rajoguna: one of the three gunas, characterized by activity, stimulation, passion and movement

Ratri: Night

Rava: Semolina

Rishi: Sage

Sadhana: Spiritual Practice

Sadhu: Ascetic

Sakshi: God's witness

Samadhi: unity with the Almighty Father; merged and engrossed in God consciousness; complete freedom from Nature's three gunas

Sankalpa: Determination; resolution; commitment

Satsang: In the company of the Divine

Sattva: The quality of tranquility, purity, virtue, illumination, balance and wisdom

Sattvic / Satogun: one of the three gunas, characterised by the qualities of God and Truth – peace, harmony, divine love, enlightenment, calmness, complete balance, self-awareness

Seva: Service

Shani: Saturn

Shanti: Peace

Siddha: Perfected, accomplished, enlightened Guru

Soham: I am That (GOD); a mantra to discover God in you.

Tamasic / Tamo / Tamoguna: one of the three qualities, charcterised by inertia, contraction and passivity

Tattva: Thatness; principle; reality; truth

Triphala: An Ayurveda formula used to enhance youthful energy, strength and vitality

Ujjai: Breath of victory

Vaishakha: the Second month of the Hindu calendar

Veena: a Stringed instrument

Vikalpa: Option; choice

Vikara: Change; transformation; modification; change of form or nature

Yagya: Ritual of sacrifice.

□□□